I0016758

POWER BI DAX

Essentials

Getting Started with Basic DAX Functions in Power BI

Kiet Huynh

Table of Contents

CHAPTER I
Introduction to DAX Essentials

1.1 Understanding Data Analysis Expressions (DAX)

Data Analysis Expressions (DAX) is a powerful formula language that is at the core of Microsoft Power BI and other Microsoft products like Excel and SQL Server Analysis Services. DAX is designed for creating custom calculations, aggregations, and data transformations within these tools. This chapter introduces you to the fundamental concepts of DAX and lays the foundation for your journey into mastering its essentials.

What is DAX?

DAX is a formula language that enables you to create custom calculations and expressions in Power BI. It provides a robust set of functions and operators that allow you to work with data and perform complex calculations on it. DAX is optimized for working with tabular data, making it ideal for data modeling and analysis.

Why DAX Matters

DAX is essential for unleashing the full potential of your data. While Power BI offers various visualizations and data manipulation tools, DAX empowers you to create sophisticated calculations that might not be possible using built-in features alone. Whether you need to perform advanced calculations, create custom metrics, or build complex business logic, DAX provides the flexibility and power to accomplish these tasks.

Basic DAX Components

DAX is composed of functions, operators, and constants. Functions are pre-built formulas that perform specific calculations, such as aggregations or date calculations. Operators, such as +, -, *, /, allow you to perform arithmetic and comparison operations. Constants are fixed values that you can use in your calculations.

Getting Started with DAX

To start using DAX, you need to understand its basic syntax. DAX formulas are written in a similar way to Excel formulas, using functions, operators, and references to columns or measures in your data model. Let's look at a simple example:

Suppose you have a Sales table with columns "Quantity" and "Unit Price." You want to create a calculated column that calculates the total sales for each row. Here's how you can write this DAX formula:

```DAX
Total Sales = Sales[Quantity] * Sales[Unit Price]
```

In this example, "Total Sales" is the name of the calculated column, and the formula multiplies the "Quantity" and "Unit Price" columns.

Working with DAX Functions

DAX offers a wide range of functions for various purposes, such as mathematical calculations, text manipulation, date and time operations, and more. Understanding how to use DAX functions is key to unlocking the potential of DAX.

For instance, you can use the SUM function to calculate the sum of values in a column:

```DAX
Total Sales = SUM(Sales[Quantity])
```

Or you can use the CONCATENATE function to combine text values:

```DAX
Full Name = CONCATENATE(Customer[First Name], " ", Customer[Last Name])
```

Summary

This chapter provided an overview of Data Analysis Expressions (DAX) and its significance in Power BI. You learned about the basic components of DAX, its syntax, and how to work with functions to perform calculations and transformations. As you delve deeper into this book, you'll explore more advanced DAX functions and techniques that will empower you to tackle complex data analysis tasks and unlock deeper insights from your data.

1.2. Importance of DAX in Power BI

Data Analysis Expressions (DAX) plays a central and pivotal role in the world of Power BI. Its significance lies in its ability to empower users to perform advanced calculations, create custom metrics, and transform data to gain deeper insights. In this section, we will delve into the key reasons why DAX is so crucial within the Power BI ecosystem.

Enabling Complex Calculations

One of the primary reasons for the importance of DAX is its capability to handle complex calculations that go beyond the built-in functionalities of Power BI. While Power BI provides various data manipulation tools and visualizations, DAX allows you to create intricate calculations tailored to your specific business needs. Whether it's calculating growth rates, creating weighted averages, or performing intricate financial analyses, DAX equips you with the tools needed to execute these tasks.

Seamless Data Transformation

DAX serves as a bridge between raw data and insightful information. Its ability to transform data on the fly allows users to perform aggregations, filtering, and restructuring operations within a single formula. For instance, you can create calculated columns or measures that summarize data based on different conditions, enabling dynamic and interactive reporting. This capability not only saves time but also enhances the efficiency of data modeling and analysis.

Enhancing Data Modeling

In Power BI, DAX goes hand-in-hand with data modeling. DAX measures and calculated columns provide a flexible way to create new dimensions, hierarchies, and relationships. By doing so, DAX enhances the analytical capabilities of your data model, allowing you to slice, dice, and drill down into your data effortlessly. This is particularly useful when dealing with large datasets and complex business structures.

Bridging the Gap between Data and Insights

DAX acts as the engine that turns data into meaningful insights. It enables users to derive valuable information from raw data, facilitating informed decision-making. With DAX, you can create key performance indicators (KPIs), ratios, and benchmarks that reflect your organization's specific goals and objectives. As a result, you can gain a deeper understanding of your data and uncover trends and patterns that might otherwise go unnoticed.

Combining Power BI Features

DAX seamlessly integrates with other features in Power BI, such as visuals, filters, and slicers. This integration allows you to build interactive dashboards and reports that respond dynamically to user interactions. You can create complex calculations and then visualize the results using various charts and graphs. The ability to combine DAX calculations with compelling visualizations empowers you to communicate insights effectively to your audience.

Conclusion

In summary, the importance of DAX in Power BI cannot be overstated. It serves as the backbone for creating sophisticated calculations, transforming data, enhancing data models, and generating valuable insights. As you continue your journey into DAX Essentials, you will delve deeper into its functionalities, exploring a variety of functions and techniques that will enable you to harness the full potential of this powerful formula language.

1.3. Getting Familiar with DAX Functions

As you embark on your journey into the world of Data Analysis Expressions (DAX), it's essential to develop a solid understanding of DAX functions—the building blocks that enable you to perform a wide range of calculations and data transformations in Power BI. In this section, we will guide you through the fundamentals of DAX functions, their syntax, and how to use them effectively.

Understanding DAX Functions

DAX functions are predefined formulas that perform specific calculations, aggregations, or transformations on your data. They are designed to be flexible and versatile, allowing you to create complex calculations with relative ease. DAX functions can be broadly categorized into several types, including mathematical, statistical, text, time intelligence, and aggregation functions, among others. Each type of function serves a unique purpose and can be combined to achieve intricate calculations.

Syntax of DAX Functions

The syntax of DAX functions consists of the function name, followed by a set of arguments enclosed in parentheses. Arguments are the inputs that the function uses to perform its calculation. The order and number of arguments can vary depending on the function. Some functions may require a single argument, while others may require multiple arguments. Understanding the syntax of DAX functions is crucial as it forms the basis for constructing your calculations.

Basic Examples of DAX Functions

Let's dive into a few basic examples of DAX functions to illustrate their usage:

1. SUM: The SUM function is used to add up the values in a specified column of a table. For instance, to calculate the total sales of a product, you can use the SUM function like this:

```
Total Sales = SUM(Sales[Amount])
```

2. AVERAGE: The AVERAGE function calculates the average of the values in a column. To find the average price of products, you can use:

```
Average Price = AVERAGE(Products[Price])
```

3. CONCATENATE: The CONCATENATE function combines text strings from multiple columns into a single text string. For example:

```
Full Name = CONCATENATE(Customers[First Name], " ", Customers[Last Name])
```

Using DAX Functions in Power BI

To use DAX functions in Power BI, follow these steps:

1. Open Power BI Desktop: Launch Power BI Desktop and load your data model.

2. Create a New Measure or Calculated Column: Go to the "Modeling" tab and click on "New Measure" or "New Calculated Column," depending on where you want to use the function.

3. Write the DAX Function: In the formula bar, type the desired DAX function, providing the necessary arguments. You can also use the "Insert Function" button to browse and select functions.

4. Evaluate and Test: Power BI provides a real-time preview of the results as you type the DAX function. Ensure that the calculated values match your expectations.

5. Save and Use: Once satisfied, save your measure or calculated column. You can now use the DAX function in visuals, tables, and other parts of your Power BI report.

Conclusion

Getting familiar with DAX functions is a fundamental step towards mastering the art of DAX. As you continue your journey through DAX Essentials, you'll explore a diverse range of functions and learn how to combine them to solve complex analytical challenges. Remember, practice is key to becoming proficient with DAX functions, so don't hesitate to experiment and apply them to your own data scenarios.

CHAPTER II
Basic DAX Functions

2.1 DAX Syntax and Structure

In Chapter 1, you gained an introduction to DAX and its significance in Power BI. Now, let's delve deeper into the world of DAX by exploring its syntax and structure. Understanding the syntax of DAX is like learning the grammar of a new language—it's essential for constructing accurate and effective calculations.

Anatomy of a DAX Formula

A DAX formula is composed of several key elements:

1. Function Name: The name of the DAX function you want to use. Functions are the building blocks of your calculations.

2. Arguments: Inputs required by the function to perform its calculation. Arguments can be column references, values, or other expressions.

3. Operators: Symbols such as +, -, *, / used to perform arithmetic and logical operations within a formula.

4. Column References: References to columns in your data model. Columns are enclosed in square brackets, e.g., `[Sales Amount]`.

5. Constants and Values: Numeric values, text strings, or logical values used directly in calculations.

6. Expressions: Combination of functions, operators, and arguments to create complex calculations.

Basic DAX Function Examples

Let's explore a few basic DAX functions to illustrate the syntax:

1. SUM: The SUM function calculates the sum of values in a column. For instance, to calculate the total sales amount, use:

```
Total Sales = SUM(Sales[Amount])
```

2. AVERAGE: The AVERAGE function computes the average of values. To find the average order quantity:

```
Average Quantity = AVERAGE(Orders[Quantity])
```

3. COUNTROWS: The COUNTROWS function counts the number of rows in a table or table expression. To count the number of products in a table:

```
Product Count = COUNTROWS(Products)
```

Applying DAX Syntax in Power BI

To create and apply DAX formulas in Power BI, follow these steps:

1. Open Power BI Desktop: Launch Power BI and load your data model.

2. Create a New Measure or Calculated Column: Navigate to the "Modeling" tab and click on "New Measure" or "New Calculated Column," depending on your needs.

3. Write the DAX Formula: In the formula bar, type the desired DAX function, arguments, and operators. Use IntelliSense for function suggestions.

4. Use Contextual Help: As you type, Power BI provides tooltips and suggestions to guide you through syntax and available functions.

5. Check for Errors: Power BI highlights syntax errors and provides error messages to help you correct any mistakes.

6. Evaluate and Test: Ensure your formula produces the expected results by referencing the corresponding visuals or tables.

7. Save and Utilize: Save your measure or calculated column. You can now use this DAX calculation in your reports and visuals.

Best Practices for DAX Syntax

Here are some best practices to keep in mind while working with DAX syntax:

1. Use Clear and Descriptive Names: Name your measures and columns in a way that reflects their purpose. This improves readability and understanding.

2. Break Down Complex Calculations: If a calculation becomes too complex, break it down into smaller, manageable steps using intermediate measures.

3. Document Your Formulas: Add comments to your DAX formulas to explain their purpose and logic. This helps others understand your calculations.

4. Test and Verify: Always test your DAX formulas with different scenarios and verify the results to ensure accuracy.

Conclusion

Mastering DAX syntax and structure is essential for effective data analysis in Power BI. In this chapter, you've learned about the components of a DAX formula and how to apply them to create basic calculations. As you progress through DAX Essentials, you'll build on this foundation and explore more advanced functions and techniques that will empower you to unlock valuable insights from your data.

2.2. Introducing DAX Functions: SUM, AVERAGE, COUNT, MIN, MAX

In the previous section, we explored the fundamental syntax and structure of DAX formulas. Now, let's dive into some of the most commonly used DAX functions: SUM, AVERAGE, COUNT, MIN, and MAX. These functions serve as the building blocks for aggregating and summarizing data in Power BI.

2.2.1 SUM Function

The SUM function is a workhorse in DAX, used to calculate the total sum of numeric values in a column. This function is particularly useful for adding up sales, revenue, or any other numerical data.

Syntax:

```
SUM(Column)
```

Example:

Suppose you have a Sales table with a column named "Sales Amount." To calculate the total sales amount, you can use the SUM function like this:

```
Total Sales Amount = SUM(Sales[Sales Amount])
```

2.2.2 AVERAGE Function

The AVERAGE function calculates the arithmetic mean of numeric values in a column. It is employed to find the average value of data, such as the average price or average rating.

Syntax:

```
AVERAGE(Column)
```

Example:

Let's say you want to determine the average price of products in a Products table. You can use the AVERAGE function as follows:

```
Average Product Price = AVERAGE(Products[Price])
```

```
```

2.2.3 COUNT Function

The COUNT function is used to count the number of rows or items in a column. It's useful for counting orders, customers, or any other categorical data.

Syntax:

```
```

COUNT(Column)

```
```

Example:

Suppose you have an Orders table and you want to count the number of orders. You can use the COUNT function like this:

```
```

Total Orders = COUNT(Orders[OrderID])

```
```

2.2.4 MIN and MAX Functions

The MIN and MAX functions determine the minimum and maximum values in a column, respectively. These functions are handy for finding the lowest and highest values in your data.

Syntax:

```
```

MIN(Column)

MAX(Column)

```
```

Example:

For instance, in a Products table, you can use the MIN and MAX functions to find the lowest and highest prices:

```
```

Lowest Price = MIN(Products[Price])

Highest Price = MAX(Products[Price])

```
```

Applying DAX Functions in Power BI

To apply these DAX functions in Power BI, follow these steps:

1. Create a New Measure: Go to the "Modeling" tab and click on "New Measure."

2. Write the DAX Formula: In the formula bar, type the desired DAX function and reference the appropriate column.

3. Evaluate and Test: Verify that the formula produces the expected result.

4. Save and Utilize: Save your measure and use it in your reports and visuals.

Best Practices for Using Basic DAX Functions

Here are some best practices to consider when using these basic DAX functions:

1. Consistent Naming: Use clear and consistent names for your measures to enhance clarity and maintainability.

2. Data Type Considerations: Ensure that the data type of the column you're referencing matches the expected data type for the function.

3. Data Context: Understand how data context affects DAX calculations and results. Learn about row context and filter context to make accurate calculations.

4. Nested Functions: You can nest these basic functions within more complex expressions to create powerful calculations.

Conclusion

In this section, you've gained a solid understanding of essential DAX functions: SUM, AVERAGE, COUNT, MIN, and MAX. These functions form the foundation of data aggregation and summarization in Power BI. As you continue your journey through DAX Essentials, you'll build upon this knowledge and explore more advanced functions and techniques to take your data analysis skills to the next level.

2.3. Applying DAX Functions in Power BI

Now that you have a grasp of some fundamental DAX functions like SUM, AVERAGE, COUNT, MIN, and MAX, it's time to put that knowledge into practice by applying these functions within Power BI. In this section, we will walk through the steps of creating measures using these DAX functions and integrating them into your Power BI reports.

2.3.1 Creating Measures in Power BI

Measures are calculated fields that perform DAX functions on your data. They allow you to perform dynamic calculations on the fly, enabling you to analyze your data in various ways without altering the underlying dataset.

Here's how you can create measures in Power BI:

1. Open Power BI Desktop: Launch Power BI Desktop and load your data source.

2. Navigate to Modeling: Click on the "Modeling" tab in the top menu.

3. Create a New Measure: Click on the "New Measure" button. A formula bar will appear at the top of the screen where you can enter your DAX formula.

2.3.2 Using DAX Functions in Measures

Let's walk through examples of how to use the DAX functions introduced earlier in your measures.

Example 1: Creating a Total Sales Measure using SUM:

Suppose you want to calculate the total sales amount from a Sales table. Follow these steps:

1. Click on New Measure: Go to the "Modeling" tab and click on "New Measure."

2. Enter the Formula: In the formula bar, type the following formula using the SUM function:

```
Total Sales = SUM(Sales[Sales Amount])
```

3. Evaluate and Test: Press Enter to evaluate the formula. Ensure that it returns the expected result.

Example 2: Calculating Average Rating using AVERAGE:

Assume you have a Ratings table with a column named "Rating." To calculate the average rating, follow these steps:

1. Click on New Measure: Create a new measure as before.

2. Write the Formula: Input the following formula using the AVERAGE function:

```
```

  Average Rating = AVERAGE(Ratings[Rating])

```
```

3. Validate the Result: Hit Enter to validate that the measure calculates the correct average rating.

2.3.3 Integrating Measures into Power BI Reports

Once you've created measures using DAX functions, you can integrate them into your Power BI reports to provide valuable insights. Here's how:

1. Build Visualizations: Add visualizations (charts, tables, etc.) to your report canvas using the fields from your dataset.

2. Drag Measures: Drag your newly created measures from the "Fields" pane to your visualizations to apply calculations.

3. Customize Visuals: Adjust visualization settings and formatting to present your data effectively.

2.3.4 Updating Measures and Iterative Refinement

As you explore and analyze your data, you might need to refine your measures or create new ones. Power BI makes it easy to iterate and improve your analyses:

1. Modify Existing Measures: To update an existing measure, go back to the formula bar, edit the formula, and press Enter to apply the changes.

2. Create Additional Measures: If you need to calculate more metrics, create new measures following the same process.

3. Test and Validate: Always validate your measures with sample data to ensure accuracy.

Best Practices for Using DAX Functions in Power BI

Here are some best practices for applying DAX functions in Power BI measures:

1. Reusability: Create measures that can be reused across multiple visualizations for consistency and efficiency.

2. Documentation: Provide clear and concise measure descriptions to aid understanding for yourself and others.

3. Organize Measures: Organize measures into logical folders to keep your model tidy as it grows.

4. Performance Considerations: Be mindful of the performance impact of complex calculations and nested functions on large datasets.

Conclusion

In this section, you've learned how to create measures using basic DAX functions and integrate them into your Power BI reports. By applying these functions and measures effectively, you can unlock deeper insights and make more informed decisions based on your data. As you continue your exploration of DAX Essentials, you'll delve into more advanced functions and techniques that will elevate your Power BI analytics to the next level.

CHAPTER III
Logical Functions in DAX

3.1 Using IF Function for Conditional Calculations

Logical functions play a crucial role in Data Analysis Expressions (DAX) by enabling you to perform calculations based on conditions or criteria. Among the essential logical functions in DAX, the IF function stands out as a versatile tool for handling conditional calculations. In this section, we will explore the IF function's syntax, usage, and provide step-by-step instructions on incorporating it into your Power BI projects.

3.1.1 Understanding the IF Function

The IF function in DAX allows you to evaluate a condition and return different values based on whether the condition is true or false. Its general syntax is as follows:

```
```

IF(LogicalTest, [ValueIfTrue], [ValueIfFalse])

```
```

- `LogicalTest`: The condition you want to test.

- `ValueIfTrue`: The value to return if the condition is true.

- `ValueIfFalse`: The value to return if the condition is false.

3.1.2 Practical Examples of Using the IF Function

Let's delve into practical scenarios where the IF function can be applied effectively.

Example 1: Categorizing Sales Data

Suppose you have a Sales table with a "Sales Amount" column, and you want to categorize each sale as "High" or "Low" based on a threshold. Here's how you can achieve this:

1. Create a New Measure: In Power BI Desktop, go to the "Modeling" tab and click "New Measure."

2. Write the Formula: Use the IF function to create the measure:

```
Sales Category = IF(Sales[Sales Amount] > 1000, "High", "Low")
```

This formula checks if the sales amount is greater than 1000. If true, it assigns the category "High"; otherwise, it assigns "Low."

3. Apply the Measure: Drag the "Sales Category" measure to a table or visualization to see the categorized sales.

Example 2: Calculating Bonus

Imagine you have an Employee table with a "Salary" column, and you want to calculate a bonus for employees earning above a certain threshold. Here's how:

1. Create a New Measure: Generate a new measure using the IF function:

```
Bonus = IF(Employee[Salary] > 50000, Employee[Salary] * 0.1, 0)
```

This formula calculates a 10% bonus for employees with a salary over $50,000.

2. Visualize the Results: Add a visual to display the calculated bonus for each employee.

3.1.3 Nested IF Functions for Complex Conditions

You can nest multiple IF functions within each other to handle more intricate conditions.

Example: Classifying Student Performance

Suppose you want to categorize student scores into "Excellent," "Good," "Average," or "Below Average." You can use nested IF functions like this:

1. Create a New Measure: Define a measure using nested IF functions:

```
```
Performance Category =
IF(Student[Scores] >= 90, "Excellent",
  IF(Student[Scores] >= 80, "Good",
    IF(Student[Scores] >= 70, "Average",
      "Below Average"
)
)
)
```
```

This formula categorizes scores based on predefined thresholds.

2. Visualize the Results: Use a visualization to display the performance categories for each student.

3.1.4 Error Handling with the IF Function

The IF function can also be used for error handling. For instance, you can replace error values with custom messages.

Example: Handling Division by Zero

Suppose you're calculating a ratio, and there's a possibility of division by zero. You can address this using the IF function:

1. Create a New Measure: Develop a measure with the IF function to handle division by zero:

```

Ratio = IF(Denominator <> 0, Numerator / Denominator, "N/A")

```

Here, if the denominator is not zero, it calculates the ratio; otherwise, it displays "N/A."

2. Include the Measure: Integrate the "Ratio" measure into a visualization.

Conclusion

The IF function in DAX empowers you to make dynamic calculations based on conditions. By understanding its syntax and practical applications, you can enhance your Power BI reports with meaningful insights. In this section, we explored the basics of the IF function and provided real-world examples to guide you through its usage. As you continue your journey into DAX Essentials, you'll uncover more advanced logical functions that open the door to even more sophisticated calculations and analyses.

3.2. Utilizing SWITCH for Advanced Logical Operations

The SWITCH function in Data Analysis Expressions (DAX) is a powerful tool for performing complex logical operations. While the IF function is ideal for simple conditions, the SWITCH function enables you to handle multiple conditions with ease. In this section, we will dive deep into the syntax, applications, and step-by-step implementation of the SWITCH function in Power BI.

3.2.1 Understanding the SWITCH Function

The SWITCH function evaluates an expression against a series of values and returns a corresponding result when a match is found. Its structure is as follows:

```
```
SWITCH(Expression, Value1, Result1, Value2, Result2, ..., [DefaultResult])
```
```

- `Expression`: The value you want to evaluate.

- `Value1`, `Value2`, etc.: Possible values to compare against the expression.

- `Result1`, `Result2`, etc.: Corresponding results to return if a match is found.

- `[DefaultResult]`: An optional default result to return if no match is found.

3.2.2 Applying SWITCH for Categorization

Let's explore a scenario where the SWITCH function can be applied effectively.

Example: Categorizing Products

Suppose you have a Product table with a "Category" column, and you want to create a new column categorizing products based on their categories using the SWITCH function.

1. Add a New Column: In Power BI Desktop, go to the "Modeling" tab and click "New Column."

2. Write the Formula: Utilize the SWITCH function to create the new column:

```
Categorized =
SWITCH(
  Product[Category],
  "Electronics", "Tech Products",
  "Clothing", "Fashion Items",
  "Groceries", "Food Essentials",
  "Books", "Literary Works",
  "Other"
)
```

This formula categorizes products based on their respective categories.

3. Incorporate the New Column: Drag the "Categorized" column into a table or visualization to see the products' categorization.

3.2.3 Complex Scenarios with SWITCH

The SWITCH function is particularly useful for handling scenarios with intricate conditions.

Example: Tiered Pricing

Imagine you want to apply tiered pricing based on the quantity of items purchased. You can use the SWITCH function to achieve this:

1. Create a New Measure: Generate a measure using the SWITCH function:

```
Tiered Price =
SWITCH(
   TRUE(),
   Sales[Quantity] >= 100, Sales[TotalAmount] * 0.9,
   Sales[Quantity] >= 50, Sales[TotalAmount] * 0.95,
   Sales[TotalAmount]
)
```

This formula applies different discounts based on the purchased quantity.

2. Visualize the Results: Add a visual to display the calculated tiered prices for each transaction.

3.2.4 Combining SWITCH with Other Functions

The SWITCH function can be combined with other DAX functions to achieve more advanced calculations.

Example: Advanced Product Categorization

Continuing from the previous example, suppose you want to further categorize products based on both their category and price range:

1. Create a New Column: Add another new column in Power BI Desktop.

2. Write the Formula: Utilize the SWITCH function along with other DAX functions:
```
```

```
Advanced Categorized =

SWITCH(

  TRUE(),

  AND(Product[Category] = "Electronics", Product[Price] > 500), "High-End Electronics",

  AND(Product[Category] = "Clothing", Product[Price] > 100), "Premium Clothing",

  [Categorized]

)

```

This formula considers both category and price range for advanced categorization.

3. Incorporate the New Column: Use the "Advanced Categorized" column in your visualizations.

Conclusion

The SWITCH function is a valuable addition to your DAX toolkit when dealing with intricate logical operations. In this section, we explored the syntax and practical applications of the SWITCH function through real-world examples. By mastering the SWITCH function, you can efficiently handle complex categorization, tiered pricing, and other advanced scenarios in your Power BI projects. As you continue your journey in understanding DAX Essentials, you'll find that logical functions like SWITCH are essential for performing dynamic calculations and transforming your data into actionable insights.

3.3. Combining Logical Functions for Complex Analysis

In the previous sections, we explored individual logical functions like IF and SWITCH, understanding how they can be used to make conditional calculations and perform advanced logical operations. However, real-world scenarios often require more complex analysis that involves multiple conditions and criteria. This is where the power of combining logical functions in Data Analysis Expressions (DAX) comes into play. By using multiple logical functions together, you can create intricate and precise calculations that yield valuable insights from your data. In this section, we'll delve into the process of combining logical functions for complex analysis in DAX, providing examples and step-by-step guidance.

3.3.1 The Need for Combining Logical Functions

Combining logical functions is essential when you need to evaluate multiple conditions simultaneously and derive insights based on various criteria. Whether you're dealing with sales data, customer behavior, or any other dataset, the ability to create compound conditions enhances your analytical capabilities.

3.3.2 Example: Customer Segmentation

Let's consider an example of customer segmentation, where we want to categorize customers based on their purchase history and location. We'll combine the IF and SWITCH functions to achieve this:

Scenario: Categorizing customers into "High-Value," "Mid-Value," and "Low-Value" segments based on their total purchase amount and location.

Steps:

1. Create a New Column: In Power BI Desktop, go to the "Modeling" tab and click "New Column."

2. Write the Formula: Combine the IF and SWITCH functions for customer segmentation:

```
```

Customer Segment =

```
IF(

  Sales[TotalAmount] > 1000,

  SWITCH(

    TRUE(),

    Sales[Location] = "New York", "High-Value",

    Sales[Location] = "Los Angeles", "High-Value",

    "Mid-Value"

  ),

  "Low-Value"

)
```
```

This formula categorizes customers into different segments based on their purchase amount and location.

**3. Visualize the Results:** Use the "Customer Segment" column in visualizations to see the segmentation of customers.

### 3.3.3 Enhancing Analysis with Nested Logical Functions

Nested logical functions involve using one logical function inside another. This approach allows you to build more sophisticated conditions and obtain granular insights.

**Example: Product Recommendations**

Imagine you want to recommend products to customers based on their purchase history and preferences. Here, we'll use nested IF statements to achieve this:
```

Scenario: Recommending products based on customers' purchase history and product category preferences.

Steps:

1. Create a New Measure: Generate a measure for product recommendations:

```
```

Product Recommendation =
IF(
  COUNTROWS(
    FILTER(
      Sales,
      Sales[CustomerID] = SELECTEDVALUE(Sales[CustomerID]) &&
      Sales[Category] = "Electronics"
)
) > 0,
  "Tech Gadgets",
  IF(
    COUNTROWS(
      FILTER(
        Sales,
        Sales[CustomerID] = SELECTEDVALUE(Sales[CustomerID]) &&
        Sales[Category] = "Clothing"
)
) > 0,
```
```

```
        "Fashion Items",

        "Explore Other Categories"

    )

  )

  ```
```

This measure recommends products based on purchase history and preferences.

2. Visualize the Results: Use the "Product Recommendation" measure in visuals to display personalized product recommendations for customers.

Conclusion

Combining logical functions in DAX empowers you to perform advanced and intricate analysis on your data. By integrating functions like IF and SWITCH, and incorporating nested functions, you can create highly tailored calculations that provide valuable insights. In this section, we explored the significance of combining logical functions and provided practical examples to illustrate the concept. As you continue your journey with DAX Essentials, mastering the art of combining logical functions will enable you to unlock the full potential of your data and drive informed decision-making in your Power BI projects.
```

CHAPTER IV
Text and String Functions

4.1 CONCATENATE and RELATED Functions for Text Manipulation

In the world of data analysis and visualization, text manipulation plays a crucial role. Being able to combine, extract, and format text strings allows you to organize and present information effectively. In this chapter, we will delve into two essential text and string functions in Data Analysis Expressions (DAX): CONCATENATE and RELATED. These functions enable you to manipulate text values in various ways, facilitating better data presentation and analysis. Let's explore how to use CONCATENATE and RELATED functions step by step, along with practical examples.

4.1.1 CONCATENATE: Combining Text Strings

The CONCATENATE function in DAX allows you to join multiple text strings together. It is particularly useful when you want to create custom labels, titles, or descriptions by combining text from different columns.

Example: Creating Full Names

Let's say you have a dataset with separate columns for first names and last names, and you want to create a column for full names.

Steps:

1. Create a New Column: In Power BI Desktop, navigate to the "Modeling" tab and select "New Column."

2. Write the Formula: Use the CONCATENATE function to combine first names and last names:

```
```

Full Name = CONCATENATE(Customer[First Name], " ", Customer[Last Name])

```
```

This formula combines the first name and last name columns with a space in between.

3. Visualize the Results: Utilize the "Full Name" column in visualizations to display the complete names of customers.

4.1.2 RELATED: Accessing Text from Related Tables

The RELATED function allows you to retrieve data from related tables. While it's often used for numeric values, you can also use it to access text or string values from related tables.

Example: Displaying Customer City

Consider a scenario where you have two tables: "Customers" and "Cities." The "Customers" table contains customer information, while the "Cities" table includes city names and related customer IDs.

Steps:

1. Create a New Column: In Power BI Desktop, go to the "Modeling" tab and choose "New Column."

2. Write the Formula: Use the RELATED function to access the city name from the "Cities" table:

```
```

```
Customer City = RELATED(Cities[CityName])
```
```

```

This formula retrieves the city name associated with each customer.

3. Visualize the Results: Utilize the "Customer City" column in visuals to display the cities of customers.

4.1.3 Handling Empty or Missing Values

When working with text manipulation, it's important to consider cases where values are missing or empty. You can use the IF function to handle such situations.

Example: Handling Missing Titles

Suppose you have a dataset of employees with titles, but some entries are missing titles. You want to replace the missing titles with a default text.

Steps:

1. Create a New Column: In Power BI Desktop, navigate to the "Modeling" tab and select "New Column."

2. Write the Formula: Use the IF function to check if the title is empty and provide a default text if it is:
```

```
```
Employee Title = IF(ISBLANK(Employee[Title]), "Unknown", Employee[Title])
```
```

```

This formula checks if the title is blank and replaces it with "Unknown."

3. Visualize the Results: Utilize the "Employee Title" column in visuals to display the titles of employees with the "Unknown" default for missing values.

Conclusion

The CONCATENATE and RELATED functions in DAX offer powerful tools for text manipulation and data organization. By combining text strings and accessing related text values, you can enhance the presentation and analysis of your data. In this chapter, we explored the step-by-step process of using CONCATENATE and RELATED functions, along with practical examples. As you continue your journey with DAX Essentials, mastering these text and string functions will enable you to efficiently manage and transform textual data, ultimately leading to more insightful and impactful visualizations and analyses in your Power BI projects.

4.2. Working with LEFT, RIGHT, and MID Functions

In this chapter, we'll dive into the versatile text and string functions available in Data Analysis Expressions (DAX): LEFT, RIGHT, and MID. These functions allow you to extract specific portions of text strings, which is crucial for data manipulation and analysis. Whether you need to isolate characters from the beginning, end, or middle of a string, these functions have you covered. Let's explore each function's usage, syntax, and practical examples to better understand their capabilities.

4.2.1 LEFT Function: Extracting Characters from the Beginning

The LEFT function in DAX enables you to extract a specified number of characters from the beginning of a text string.

Example: Extracting Country Codes

Imagine you have a dataset with product codes that include two-character country codes at the beginning. You want to extract these country codes.

Steps:

1. Create a New Column: Open your Power BI Desktop project and navigate to the "Modeling" tab. Select "New Column."

2. Write the Formula: Use the LEFT function to extract the first two characters from the product code:

```
Country Code = LEFT(Product[ProductCode], 2)
```

This formula extracts the first two characters from the "ProductCode" column.

3. Visualize the Results: Use the "Country Code" column in visuals to display the extracted country codes.

4.2.2 RIGHT Function: Extracting Characters from the End

The RIGHT function allows you to extract a specified number of characters from the end of a text string.

Example: Extracting File Extensions

Suppose you have a dataset containing filenames, and you want to extract the file extensions.

Steps:

1. Create a New Column: In Power BI Desktop, navigate to the "Modeling" tab and select "New Column."

2. Write the Formula: Use the RIGHT function to extract the last three characters from the filename:

```
```

```
File Extension = RIGHT(Files[FileName], 3)
```

```
```

This formula extracts the last three characters from the "FileName" column.

3. Visualize the Results: Utilize the "File Extension" column in visuals to display the extracted file extensions.

4.2.3 MID Function: Extracting Characters from the Middle

The MID function enables you to extract a specified number of characters from the middle of a text string, starting from a given position.

Example: Extracting Product Codes

Consider a dataset with product codes, and you want to extract the middle portion of the codes.

Steps:

1. Create a New Column: Open your Power BI project and go to the "Modeling" tab. Choose "New Column."

2. Write the Formula: Use the MID function to extract characters from the middle of the product code:

```
```

Middle Code = MID(Product[ProductCode], 3, 4)

```
```

This formula starts from the third character and extracts the next four characters from the "ProductCode" column.

3. Visualize the Results: Utilize the "Middle Code" column in visuals to display the extracted middle portions of the product codes.

4.2.4 Handling Varying Text Lengths

When working with text extraction, it's important to consider cases where text lengths vary. You can use the IF function to address such situations.

Example: Handling Short Product Codes

Suppose you have a dataset of product codes, and some codes are shorter than others. You want to pad the shorter codes with zeros to make them uniform.

Steps:

1. Create a New Column: In Power BI Desktop, navigate to the "Modeling" tab and select "New Column."

2. Write the Formula: Use the IF function to check the length of the product code and pad it with zeros if needed:

```
```

Padded Code = IF(LEN(Product[ProductCode]) < 8, CONCATENATE("00", Product[ProductCode]), Product[ProductCode])

```
```

This formula checks if the length of the code is less than eight characters and adds "00" in front if necessary.

3. Visualize the Results: Utilize the "Padded Code" column in visuals to display the modified product codes.

Conclusion

The LEFT, RIGHT, and MID functions in DAX offer powerful tools for extracting specific portions of text strings. By leveraging these functions, you can manipulate and analyze textual data in a precise and structured manner. In this chapter, we explored the step-by-step process of working with these functions, along with practical examples. As you continue your journey with DAX Essentials, mastering these text and string functions will empower you to efficiently manage and transform text-based data, enabling you to create more insightful and meaningful visualizations and analyses in your Power BI projects.

4.3. Formatting and Cleaning Text Data with DAX

In the realm of data analysis and visualization, having clean and well-formatted text data is essential. The ability to format and clean text data efficiently is crucial for enhancing the quality of your analysis and ensuring accurate insights. In this section, we will delve into how you can use Data Analysis Expressions (DAX) functions to format and clean text data effectively in Power BI.

4.3.1 Changing Text Case

DAX provides functions to convert text to different cases: UPPER, LOWER, and PROPER.

Example: Converting Text to Upper Case

Let's say you have a dataset containing product names, and you want to convert them to upper case for consistency.

Steps:

1. Create a New Column: Open your Power BI project and navigate to the "Modeling" tab. Select "New Column."

2. Write the Formula: Use the UPPER function to convert product names to upper case:

```
Product Name Upper = UPPER(Product[ProductName])
```

This formula converts all characters in the "ProductName" column to upper case.

3. Visualize the Results: Utilize the "Product Name Upper" column in visuals to display the converted product names.

4.3.2 Removing Unwanted Characters

DAX functions such as SUBSTITUTE and TRIM can help remove specific characters or extra spaces from text.

Example: Removing Currency Symbols

Suppose you have a dataset with sales data that includes currency symbols in the revenue column, and you want to remove these symbols.

Steps:

1. Create a New Column: In Power BI Desktop, navigate to the "Modeling" tab and select "New Column."

2. Write the Formula: Use the SUBSTITUTE function to remove currency symbols from the revenue values:

```
```

Revenue Cleaned = SUBSTITUTE(Sales[Revenue], "$", "")

```
```

This formula replaces the dollar sign with an empty string in the "Revenue" column.

3. Visualize the Results: Utilize the "Revenue Cleaned" column in visuals to display the cleaned revenue values.

4.3.3 Extracting Substrings with FIND and SEARCH

The FIND and SEARCH functions in DAX allow you to locate the position of a substring within a text string and extract a portion of the text.

Example: Extracting Domain Names

Consider a dataset with email addresses, and you want to extract the domain names.

Steps:

1. Create a New Column: Open your Power BI project and go to the "Modeling" tab. Choose "New Column."

2. Write the Formula: Use the FIND function to locate the position of the "@" symbol and the RIGHT function to extract the domain name:

```
```

Domain Name = RIGHT(UserData[EmailAddress], LEN(UserData[EmailAddress]) - FIND("@", UserData[EmailAddress]))

```
```

This formula extracts the portion of the email address after the "@" symbol.

3. Visualize the Results: Utilize the "Domain Name" column in visuals to display the extracted domain names.

4.3.4 Cleaning Whitespace

Extra spaces in text data can lead to inaccuracies in analysis. The TRIM function can help remove leading and trailing spaces.

Example: Cleaning Product Names

Suppose you have a dataset with product names that have inconsistent spacing, and you want to clean them.

Steps:

1. Create a New Column: In Power BI Desktop, navigate to the "Modeling" tab and select "New Column."

2. Write the Formula: Use the TRIM function to remove leading and trailing spaces from product names:

```
Cleaned Product Name = TRIM(Product[ProductName])
```

This formula removes extra spaces from the beginning and end of the "ProductName" column.

3. Visualize the Results: Utilize the "Cleaned Product Name" column in visuals to display the cleaned product names.

Conclusion

In this chapter, we explored how to format and clean text data using various DAX functions. From changing text case to removing unwanted characters and cleaning whitespace, DAX provides a range of powerful tools for enhancing the quality and accuracy of your data analysis. By following the practical examples and step-by-step instructions provided, you can effectively apply these text and string functions to your Power BI projects. Clean and well-formatted text data will contribute to more reliable insights and visualizations, ultimately leading to better-informed decision-making processes.

CHAPTER V
Date and Time Functions

5.1 Understanding Date and Time in DAX

In the world of data analysis, working with date and time information is a fundamental aspect. Dates and times are ubiquitous in datasets, and being able to manipulate and analyze them effectively is crucial for deriving meaningful insights. Data Analysis Expressions (DAX) offers a comprehensive set of functions to handle date and time data, enabling you to perform calculations, comparisons, and aggregations based on temporal information. In this chapter, we will delve into the intricacies of date and time functions in DAX, providing you with a solid foundation to harness the power of temporal data in your Power BI projects.

5.1.1 The Importance of Date and Time

Date and time data provide context to your analyses. Whether you're examining sales trends, customer behavior, or financial performance, understanding when events occurred is essential. For instance, you may want to know the total sales for a particular month, the average number of orders per day, or the year-over-year growth rate. DAX date and time functions empower you to answer these questions and more, enabling you to gain deeper insights into your data.

5.1.2 Date and Time Formats

Before delving into DAX date and time functions, it's essential to grasp the common date and time formats. In Power BI, date and time values are often stored in the "datetime" format, which includes both date and time components. The date component consists of the year, month, and day, while the time component includes hours, minutes, seconds, and fractions of a second. These values are usually represented in a recognizable format, such as "YYYY-MM-DD hh:mm:ss," making them human-readable and usable for analysis.

5.1.3 Handling Time Zones

Dealing with time zones is a critical consideration when working with date and time data from various sources. Power BI automatically converts date and time values to your local time zone, ensuring consistency across visuals and reports. However, if you need to analyze data in different time zones, you can use DAX functions like CONVERT and AT TIME ZONE to make necessary adjustments.

5.1.4 Basic Date and Time Functions

DAX offers an array of functions to work with date and time data. Some of the basic functions include:

- **TODAY():** Returns the current date.

- **NOW():** Returns the current date and time.

- **DATE(year, month, day):** Creates a date value from the provided components.

- **TIME(hour, minute, second):** Creates a time value from the provided components.

Example: Calculating Days to Today

Suppose you have a dataset with project deadlines, and you want to calculate the number of days remaining until each project is due.

Steps:

1. Create a New Column: In Power BI Desktop, navigate to the "Modeling" tab and select "New Column."

2. Write the Formula: Use the DATEDIFF function to calculate the difference in days between the project deadline and today's date:

```
```

```
Days to Deadline = DATEDIFF('Projects'[Deadline], TODAY(), DAY)
```

```
```

This formula computes the number of days remaining for each project.

3. Visualize the Results: Utilize the "Days to Deadline" column in visuals to monitor project timelines.

Understanding date and time functions in DAX equips you with the tools to perform various calculations and analyses based on temporal data. By mastering these functions, you'll be able to uncover trends, patterns, and insights that drive better decision-making and enhance your data-driven narratives.

5.2. Using DATE, YEAR, MONTH, and DAY Functions

In the realm of data analysis, understanding and manipulating date and time data are crucial for insightful insights. In this section, we will explore how to use some fundamental DAX functions – DATE, YEAR, MONTH, and DAY – to extract specific components from date values. These functions can be particularly useful when you need to analyze data trends, patterns, and behaviors based on different date parts.

5.2.1 Extracting Year, Month, and Day

Often, you need to break down dates into their individual components for a more detailed analysis. The YEAR, MONTH, and DAY functions allow you to extract these components from a date and perform calculations based on them.

Example 1: Extracting Year from Dates

Suppose you have a dataset containing sales records, and you want to analyze sales trends based on years.

Steps:

1. Create a New Column: Navigate to the "Modeling" tab in Power BI Desktop and select "New Column."

2. Write the Formula: Use the YEAR function to extract the year from the sales date:

```
Sales Year = YEAR('Sales'[SalesDate])
```

This formula creates a new column that contains the year for each sales record.

3. Visualize the Results: Utilize the "Sales Year" column in visuals to analyze sales trends on a yearly basis.

Example 2: Extracting Month from Dates

Suppose you want to examine the distribution of sales across different months.

Steps:

1. Create a New Column: In Power BI, navigate to the "Modeling" tab and select "New Column."

2. Write the Formula: Use the MONTH function to extract the month from the sales date:

```
Sales Month = MONTH('Sales'[SalesDate])
```

This formula creates a new column that contains the month number for each sales record.

3. Visualize the Results: Utilize the "Sales Month" column in visuals to analyze sales distribution across different months.

Example 3: Extracting Day from Dates

Suppose you want to analyze sales patterns based on the day of the month.

Steps:

1. Create a New Column: In Power BI Desktop, navigate to the "Modeling" tab and select "New Column."

2. Write the Formula: Use the DAY function to extract the day from the sales date:

```
```

Sales Day = DAY('Sales'[SalesDate])

```
```

This formula creates a new column that contains the day of the month for each sales record.

3. Visualize the Results: Utilize the "Sales Day" column in visuals to analyze sales patterns based on days of the month.

5.2.2 Using the DATE Function

The DATE function is powerful for creating new date values by specifying the year, month, and day components.

Example: Calculating Future Dates

Suppose you want to calculate the delivery date for orders, which is 7 days after the order date.

Steps:

1. Create a New Column: In Power BI, navigate to the "Modeling" tab and select "New Column."

2. Write the Formula: Use the DATE function to calculate the delivery date by adding 7 days to the order date:

```
```

Delivery Date = 'Orders'[OrderDate] + 7

```
```

This formula creates a new column with the delivery dates.

3. Visualize the Results: Utilize the "Delivery Date" column in visuals to analyze delivery patterns.

5.2.3 Working with Time Intervals

Besides extracting components from date values, you can also work with time intervals using the DATEDIFF function.

Example: Calculating Age

Suppose you have a dataset with customer birthdates, and you want to calculate their ages.

Steps:

1. Create a New Column: Navigate to the "Modeling" tab in Power BI Desktop and select "New Column."

2. Write the Formula: Use the DATEDIFF function to calculate the difference in years between the current date and the birthdate:
```
```
Age = DATEDIFF('Customers'[Birthdate], TODAY(), YEAR)
```
```

This formula calculates the ages of customers based on their birthdates.

3. Visualize the Results: Utilize the "Age" column in visuals to analyze the distribution of customer ages.

By effectively using the DATE, YEAR, MONTH, and DAY functions, you can gain valuable insights from your date and time data in Power BI, enabling you to make informed decisions and discover trends that might otherwise go unnoticed.

5.3. Calculating Time-Based Metrics with DAX

Time-based metrics are essential for understanding trends, performance, and behaviors over different time periods. Data Analysis Expressions (DAX) provides a robust set of functions to calculate a wide range of time-based metrics, enabling you to gain deeper insights into your data. In this section, we will explore various scenarios where DAX functions can be used to calculate meaningful time-based metrics in Power BI.

5.3.1 Cumulative Metrics

Cumulative metrics allow you to track the accumulation of a quantity over time. One common use case is calculating cumulative sales, which provides insights into revenue growth. The **TOTALYTD** function is particularly useful for this purpose. It calculates the total of a measure from the beginning of the year to a specified date.

Example: Calculating Year-to-Date Sales

Suppose you have a sales dataset with a "Sales" column and a "Date" column. You want to calculate the cumulative sales for each month.

Steps:

1. Create a New Measure: In Power BI Desktop, navigate to the "Modeling" tab and select "New Measure."

2. Write the Formula: Use the TOTALYTD function to calculate the year-to-date cumulative sales:

```
```
YTD Sales = TOTALYTD(SUM('Sales'[Sales]), 'Date'[Date])
```
```

This formula sums the "Sales" column from the beginning of the year to the specified date.

3. Visualize the Results: Add the "YTD Sales" measure to a visual, such as a line chart, to observe the cumulative sales trend over time.

5.3.2 Period-over-Period Comparison

Period-over-period comparisons help you analyze data changes between different time periods, such as months, quarters, or years. The SAMEPERIODLASTYEAR function enables you to compare metrics with the same period in the previous year.

Example: Comparing Monthly Sales with Previous Year

Continuing with the sales dataset, you want to compare the sales for each month with the corresponding month in the previous year.

Steps:

1. Create a New Measure: Create a new measure to calculate the total sales for the current year:

```
Current Year Sales = SUM('Sales'[Sales])
```

2. Write the Formula: Use the SAMEPERIODLASTYEAR function to calculate the sales for the same period in the previous year:

```
PY Sales = CALCULATE([Current Year Sales], SAMEPERIODLASTYEAR('Date'[Date]))
```

This formula calculates the sales for the same period (month) in the previous year.

3. Calculate the Difference: Create another measure to calculate the difference between the current year's sales and the previous year's sales:

```
YoY Sales Difference = [Current Year Sales] - [PY Sales]
```

4. Visualize the Results: Use visuals like a column chart to display the year-over-year sales difference.

5.3.3 Moving Averages

Moving averages smooth out fluctuations in data by calculating the average of a specific number of preceding and succeeding data points. The AVERAGEX and EARLIER functions are handy for calculating moving averages.

Example: Calculating 3-Month Moving Average

Suppose you want to calculate the 3-month moving average of sales to identify trends over time.

Steps:

1. Create a New Measure: Create a new measure to calculate the moving average:

```
3-Month Moving Avg =
AVERAGEX(
  FILTER(
    ALL('Date'),
    'Date'[Date] <= MAX('Date'[Date]) &&
    'Date'[Date] >= MAX('Date'[Date]) - 90
  ),
  [Current Year Sales]
)
```

2. Visualize the Results: Use a line chart to visualize the 3-month moving average alongside actual sales data.

By leveraging DAX functions, you can effortlessly compute a wide range of time-based metrics, enabling you to analyze trends, make informed decisions, and drive data-driven narratives. These examples demonstrate the versatility and power of DAX in handling temporal data and uncovering valuable insights from it.

CHAPTER VI
Aggregation and Filter Functions

6.1 Applying SUMX, AVERAGEX, and COUNTX Functions

In Power BI, data analysis often involves the need to perform calculations on aggregated values while considering specific filters or conditions. The SUMX, AVERAGEX, and COUNTX functions in Data Analysis Expressions (DAX) are powerful tools that allow you to perform such calculations by applying aggregation and filtering simultaneously. This chapter delves into the application of these functions to enhance your data analysis capabilities in Power BI.

6.1.1 Using SUMX for Aggregated Summation

The SUMX function extends the traditional SUM function by allowing you to sum up a column while applying filters to another table. This is particularly useful when you need to calculate sums based on specific conditions or relationships between tables.

Example: Calculating Total Sales for Selected Products

Suppose you have a sales dataset with a "Sales" table containing sales transactions, and a "Products" table with product information. You want to calculate the total sales for selected products.

Steps:

1. Create a New Measure: In Power BI Desktop, go to the "Modeling" tab and create a new measure.

2. Write the Formula: Use the SUMX function to calculate the total sales for selected products:

```DAX
Total Sales = SUMX('Products', RELATED('Sales'[SalesAmount]))
```

This formula iterates through each product in the "Products" table, retrieves the corresponding sales amount from the "Sales" table, and sums up the values.

3. Visualize the Results: Create a visual representation, such as a card or table, to display the total sales for the selected products.

6.1.2 AVERAGEX for Weighted Averages

The AVERAGEX function calculates the average of an expression while applying filters or conditions to another table. It is particularly useful for computing weighted averages where each value has a specific weight.

Example: Computing Weighted Average Ratings

Suppose you have a "Movies" dataset with a "Ratings" table containing movie ratings and a "Movies" table with movie details. You want to calculate the weighted average ratings for movies based on the number of votes.

Steps:

1. Create a New Measure: Create a new measure to calculate the weighted average ratings:

```DAX
```

```
Weighted Avg Rating =
AVERAGEX(
    'Movies',
    'Movies'[Rating] * 'Movies'[Votes]
)
```
```

This formula multiplies each movie's rating by the number of votes and calculates the average of the results.

**2. Visualize the Results:** Use a visual like a card or table to display the weighted average ratings for movies.

### 6.1.3 COUNTX for Filtered Count

The COUNTX function counts the number of rows in a table that meet specific conditions, enabling you to perform filtered counts based on related tables.

**Example: Counting the Number of High-Value Customers**

Continuing with the sales dataset, you want to count the number of high-value customers who made purchases above a certain threshold.

**Steps:**

**1. Create a New Measure:** Create a measure to count the number of high-value customers:

```DAX

```
High-Value Customers =
COUNTX(
    FILTER('Customers', 'Customers'[TotalPurchases] > 1000),
    'Customers'[CustomerID]
)
```
```

This formula filters the "Customers" table to include only customers with total purchases above $1000 and counts the rows.

2. Visualize the Results: Visualize the count of high-value customers using a card or any other appropriate visual.

By mastering the application of SUMX, AVERAGEX, and COUNTX functions, you gain the ability to perform advanced aggregations and calculations while considering specific filters or conditions. These functions significantly enhance your data analysis capabilities in Power BI, enabling you to uncover insights that may otherwise go unnoticed. As you continue your journey in Power BI, keep these functions in your toolbox for versatile and insightful data analysis.

6.2. Utilizing FILTER to Modify Context in DAX

In Data Analysis Expressions (DAX), the FILTER function plays a crucial role in modifying the filter context of a calculation. By using FILTER, you can control which data is considered for calculations, thereby allowing you to perform more targeted analyses. This chapter focuses on the practical applications of the FILTER function to enhance your understanding and proficiency in Power BI.

6.2.1 Understanding the FILTER Function
```

The FILTER function allows you to create a new table by applying one or more filters to an existing table. This new table then becomes the basis for calculations, altering the filter context and enabling more precise analyses.

Example: Calculating Average Sales for Specific Product Categories

Suppose you have a "Sales" table with sales transactions and a "Products" table with product information. You want to calculate the average sales for specific product categories.

Steps:

1. Create a New Measure: Begin by creating a new measure to calculate the average sales for specific product categories:

```DAX
Average Sales by Category =
AVERAGEX(
    FILTER('Products', 'Products'[Category] = "Electronics"),
    'Sales'[SalesAmount]
)
```

This formula uses the FILTER function to create a new table containing only rows from the "Products" table where the category is "Electronics." The AVERAGEX function then calculates the average sales for this filtered context.

2. Modify the Filter Criteria: You can modify the filter criteria to calculate the average sales for other product categories. For example:

```DAX
```

Average Sales by Clothing =

AVERAGEX(

    FILTER('Products', 'Products'[Category] = "Clothing"),

    'Sales'[SalesAmount]

)

```

**3. Visualize the Results:** Use visualizations such as cards or tables to display the average sales for different product categories.

### 6.2.2 Combining FILTER with Other Functions

FILTER can be combined with other DAX functions to perform more complex calculations and analyses. For instance, you can combine it with COUNTX to count specific occurrences within a filtered context.

**Example: Counting High-Value Customers for Each Product Category**

Continuing with the sales dataset, let's count the number of high-value customers who made purchases above $1000 for each product category.

**Steps:**

**1. Create a New Measure:** Create a new measure to count high-value customers for each product category:

    ```DAX

High-Value Customers by Category =

COUNTX(

    FILTER('Customers', 'Customers'[TotalPurchases] > 1000),

    'Sales'[CustomerID]

)

```

This formula uses the FILTER function to create a new table with high-value customers and counts the occurrences of each customer ID within that context.

2. Visualize the Results: Visualize the count of high-value customers for each product category using appropriate visuals.

6.2.3 Using FILTER to Remove Filters

In some scenarios, you may want to temporarily remove filters from a calculation to ensure that it operates in a different context. The FILTER function can be used to remove filters and achieve this result.

Example: Calculating Total Sales Regardless of Filters

Suppose you want to calculate the total sales for all products without considering any active filters.

Steps:

1. Create a New Measure: Create a measure to calculate total sales regardless of filters:
```

```DAX
Total Sales (No Filters) =
SUMX(
    ALL('Products'),
    'Sales'[SalesAmount]
)
```

The FILTER function is not explicitly used here, but the ALL function is employed to remove all filters from the 'Products' table.

2. Visualize the Results: Display the total sales without filters using a suitable visual.

By mastering the utilization of the FILTER function, you gain the ability to control and modify the filter context of your calculations. This flexibility enhances your data analysis capabilities in Power BI, enabling you to perform targeted and contextually relevant analyses that provide deeper insights into your data. Experiment with FILTER in combination with other DAX functions to unlock even more advanced analytical possibilities in your Power BI projects.

6.3. Combining Aggregation and Filter Functions for Dynamic Analysis

In the realm of Data Analysis Expressions (DAX), the fusion of aggregation and filter functions empowers analysts and data professionals to perform dynamic analyses that adapt to changing contexts. This chapter delves into the strategic integration of aggregation functions like SUMX, AVERAGEX, and COUNTX with filter functions to create dynamic calculations that respond to user interactions and selections in Power BI.

6.3.1 The Power of Dynamic Analysis

Dynamic analysis involves creating calculations that adjust based on user interactions, such as selecting specific filters or slicers in a Power BI report. This approach enables you to explore data in a more personalized and interactive manner, enhancing your ability to gain insights.

Example: Dynamic Sales Forecast

Consider a scenario where you want to create a dynamic sales forecast that allows users to select a specific region and view the projected sales for that region.

Steps:

1. Create a Measure: Begin by creating a measure to calculate the forecasted sales for the selected region:

```DAX
Dynamic Sales Forecast =
SUMX(
    FILTER('Sales', 'Sales'[Region] = SELECTEDVALUE('Regions'[Region])),
    'Sales'[ProjectedSales]
)
```

This formula employs the SUMX function to aggregate projected sales for the region selected by the user. The FILTER function filters the 'Sales' table to consider only the data relevant to the chosen region.

2. Use Slicers or Filters: In your Power BI report, add slicers or filters that allow users to select a specific region. As the user interacts with the slicers or filters, the Dynamic Sales Forecast measure adjusts accordingly.

3. Visualize the Results: Display the dynamic sales forecast using visuals such as cards or tables. As users change the selected region, the forecasted sales will dynamically update.

6.3.2 Implementing Multi-Stage Filtering

Another powerful application of combining aggregation and filter functions is performing multi-stage filtering for more intricate analyses. This technique allows you to apply filters sequentially, creating a cascading effect that refines the data further.

Example: Multi-Stage Filtering for Product Categories

Suppose you want to analyze sales performance for specific product categories in different regions. Users should be able to select a region and then choose from the available product categories to view detailed insights.

Steps:

1. Create Measures: Develop measures to perform multi-stage filtering for sales analysis:

```DAX
Filtered Sales =
SUMX(
    FILTER('Sales', 'Sales'[Region] = SELECTEDVALUE('Regions'[Region])),
    'Sales'[SalesAmount]
```

)

Filtered Sales by Category =

SUMX(

  FILTER('Products', 'Products'[Category] = SELECTEDVALUE('Categories'[Category])),

  [Filtered Sales]

)

```

The first measure, Filtered Sales, aggregates sales based on the selected region. The second measure, Filtered Sales by Category, takes the Filtered Sales measure and further filters it based on the chosen product category.

**2. Use Slicers or Filters:** In your report, add slicers or filters for both regions and product categories. Users can first select a region and then choose a product category for detailed analysis.

**3. Visualize the Results:** Utilize visuals to showcase the filtered sales data for the selected region and product category. Users can explore sales insights with a dynamic and multi-stage filtering approach.

### 6.3.3 Enhancing User Experience with Dynamic Analysis

When combining aggregation and filter functions for dynamic analysis, consider enhancing the user experience by incorporating visuals and interactions that facilitate exploration.

**Example: Dynamic Sales Growth Analysis**
```

Imagine you want to enable users to analyze sales growth over different time periods dynamically. Users should be able to select a time period (month, quarter, year) and view the sales growth for that period.

Steps:

1. Create a Measure: Develop a measure to calculate sales growth dynamically:

```DAX
Dynamic Sales Growth =
DIVIDE(
   [Total Sales],
   CALCULATE(
      [Total Sales],
      DATEADD('Calendar'[Date], -1, SELECTEDVALUE('Time Periods'[Period]))
   )
) - 1
```

This formula calculates the sales growth by comparing total sales for the selected time period with total sales for the previous time period. The DIVIDE function is used to calculate the growth percentage.

2. Use Slicers or Filters: Add slicers or filters for time periods (month, quarter, year). Users can select a specific time period for analysis.

3. Visualize the Results: Display the dynamic sales growth using visuals such as line charts. As users change the selected time period, the growth analysis will dynamically adjust.

By mastering the art of combining aggregation and filter functions for dynamic analysis, you empower yourself to create insightful and interactive reports in Power BI. Users can explore data from various perspectives, engage with the information, and gain a deeper understanding of trends and patterns. Experiment with different combinations of aggregation and filter functions to design dynamic calculations that resonate with your specific analytical objectives.

CHAPTER VII
Introduction to Tables and Iterations

7.1 Working with Tables in DAX

Tables play a crucial role in Data Analysis Expressions (DAX) as they provide the foundation for data organization, manipulation, and analysis. In this chapter, we delve into the fundamentals of working with tables in DAX, including creating tables, referencing tables, and performing basic operations. By mastering these concepts, you'll be well-equipped to harness the power of DAX for more complex data analyses and calculations.

7.1.1 Creating Tables in DAX

Creating tables in DAX allows you to define a data structure that represents your dataset. These tables serve as the building blocks for your calculations and analyses.

Example: Creating a Sales Table

Suppose you have a dataset containing sales information, including product names, dates, quantities, and sales amounts. To create a table named 'Sales' in DAX, follow these steps:

1. Open Power BI Desktop: Launch Power BI Desktop and create a new report.

2. Modeling Tab: Navigate to the Modeling tab in the Power BI ribbon.

3. New Table: Click on the New Table button. A formula bar will appear at the top of the screen.

4. Define Table Schema: In the formula bar, define the schema of the 'Sales' table using the following DAX syntax:

```DAX
Sales =
DATATABLE(
    "Product", STRING,
    "Date", DATE,
    "Quantity", INTEGER,
    "SalesAmount", DECIMAL,
    {
        {"ProductA", DATE(2023, 1, 1), 10, 200},
        {"ProductB", DATE(2023, 1, 2), 15, 300},
        {"ProductA", DATE(2023, 1, 2), 5, 100}
        -- Add more rows as needed
    }
)
```

This DAX formula creates a table named 'Sales' with columns for "Product," "Date," "Quantity," and "SalesAmount." It also populates the table with sample data.

5. Load Data: Press Enter to create the 'Sales' table. Power BI will prompt you to load the data. Click Load to add the table to your model.

7.1.2 Referencing Tables and Columns

Once you have created tables, you can reference their columns to perform calculations and analyses.

Example: Referencing Columns for Total Sales

Suppose you want to calculate the total sales for each product. Follow these steps:

1. Create a Measure: Navigate to the Modeling tab and click on the New Measure button.

2. Define Calculation: In the formula bar, define the calculation for total sales:

```DAX
Total Sales = SUM('Sales'[SalesAmount])
```

This DAX formula uses the SUM function to aggregate the 'SalesAmount' column in the 'Sales' table.

3. Use the Measure: Drag and drop the 'Total Sales' measure onto a visualization, such as a table or card. Power BI will display the total sales for each product.

7.1.3 Basic Table Operations

DAX provides various functions for performing basic table operations, such as filtering and sorting.

Example: Filtering a Table

Suppose you want to create a table that includes only the sales records for a specific product. Follow these steps:

1. Create a New Table: Navigate to the Modeling tab and click on the New Table button.

2. Define Filtered Table: In the formula bar, define the filtered table using the FILTER function:

```DAX
FilteredSales =
FILTER('Sales', 'Sales'[Product] = "ProductA")
```

This DAX formula creates a new table named 'FilteredSales' by filtering the 'Sales' table based on the specified product.

3. Load Data: Press Enter to create the 'FilteredSales' table and load the data.

4. Visualize Data: Drag and drop columns from the 'FilteredSales' table onto a visualization to see the filtered sales data.

Working with tables in DAX serves as the foundation for more advanced calculations and analyses. As you become proficient in creating tables, referencing columns, and performing basic operations, you'll unlock the potential to build sophisticated DAX expressions that deliver insights and drive data-driven decisions.

7.2. Using VALUES and ALL Functions for Iterations

Iterations are a powerful concept in Data Analysis Expressions (DAX) that enable you to perform calculations over a set of values or iterate through a table's rows. The VALUES and ALL functions are fundamental tools for implementing iterations in DAX. In this section, we'll explore how to leverage these functions to perform iterative calculations and gain deeper insights from your data.

7.2.1 The VALUES Function

The VALUES function returns a single-column table containing the distinct values from a specified column in a table. This function is particularly useful for aggregating data based on unique values.

Example: Calculating Total Sales for Selected Products

Suppose you want to calculate the total sales for a specific set of products. Here's how you can achieve this using the VALUES function:

1. Create a Measure: Navigate to the Modeling tab and click on the New Measure button.

2. Define Calculation: In the formula bar, define the calculation for total sales using the VALUES function:

```DAX
SelectedProductTotalSales =
SUMX(
    VALUES('Sales'[Product]),
    [Total Sales]
)
```

In this DAX formula, the VALUES function retrieves the distinct product values from the 'Sales' table. The SUMX function then calculates the total sales for each selected product.

3. Visualize Data: Drag and drop the 'SelectedProductTotalSales' measure onto a visualization, such as a card or table. You can now see the total sales for the chosen products.

7.2.2 The ALL Function

The ALL function removes any filters from a specified table or column, allowing you to perform calculations without considering the context of the current filter or slicer selection.

Example: Calculating Total Sales Without Filters

Suppose you want to calculate the total sales for all products, regardless of any filters applied to the data. Here's how you can achieve this using the ALL function:

1. Create a Measure: Navigate to the Modeling tab and click on the New Measure button.

2. Define Calculation: In the formula bar, define the calculation for total sales without filters using the ALL function:

```DAX
TotalSalesWithoutFilters =
SUMX(
    ALL('Sales'[Product]),
    [Total Sales]
)
```

This DAX formula removes filters from the 'Product' column and calculates the total sales for all products.

3. Visualize Data: Drag and drop the 'TotalSalesWithoutFilters' measure onto a visualization. The measure displays the total sales without considering any filters or slicer selections.

7.2.3 Combining VALUES and ALL for Advanced Iterations

You can combine the VALUES and ALL functions to perform even more advanced iterations and calculations.

Example: Calculating Percentage of Total Sales for Each Product

Suppose you want to calculate the percentage of total sales that each product contributes, based on the total sales for all products. Here's how you can achieve this by combining the VALUES and ALL functions:

1. Create a Measure: Navigate to the Modeling tab and click on the New Measure button.

2. Define Calculation: In the formula bar, define the calculation for percentage of total sales using the VALUES and ALL functions:

```DAX
PercentageOfTotalSales =
DIVIDE(
    [Total Sales],
    CALCULATE(
        [Total Sales],
```

```
    ALL('Sales'[Product])
  )
)
```

This DAX formula calculates the percentage of total sales for each product by dividing the total sales for the selected product by the total sales for all products.

3. Visualize Data: Drag and drop the 'PercentageOfTotalSales' measure onto a visualization. You'll see the percentage of total sales contributed by each product.

The VALUES and ALL functions provide essential capabilities for performing iterations and creating more sophisticated calculations in DAX. By mastering these functions, you'll be able to analyze data from different angles, make informed decisions, and present insights that drive business outcomes.

7.3. Creating Dynamic Tables with DAX

In Data Analysis Expressions (DAX), tables are the backbone of data modeling and analysis in Power BI. While static tables are crucial for organizing and managing data, dynamic tables offer the flexibility to create custom aggregations, perform complex calculations, and respond dynamically to user interactions. In this section, we will delve into the creation of dynamic tables using DAX, providing you with the knowledge to harness this powerful capability.

7.3.1 Generating a Basic Dynamic Table

To create a dynamic table, you can utilize DAX functions within a calculated table. This allows you to define the structure and contents of the table based on your specific requirements.

Example: Creating a Dynamic Product Category Table

Suppose you have a 'Sales' table with a 'Product' column, and you want to create a dynamic table that lists all unique product categories. Here's how you can achieve this:

1. Navigate to Data Modeling: In Power BI Desktop, navigate to the Modeling tab.

2. Create a New Table: Click on the New Table button.

3. Define Calculation: In the formula bar, define the calculation for the dynamic product category table using the DISTINCT function:

```DAX
DynamicProductCategories =
DISTINCT('Sales'[Product Category])
```

This DAX formula creates a dynamic table named 'DynamicProductCategories' that lists all unique product categories from the 'Sales' table.

4. Visualize Data: Drag and drop the 'Product Category' column from the 'DynamicProductCategories' table onto a visualization, such as a table or slicer. You can now interact with the dynamic table based on your data.

7.3.2 Incorporating Calculated Columns

Dynamic tables can also incorporate calculated columns that enhance the analysis and visualization of data.

Example: Calculating Profit Margin in a Dynamic Product Table

Building upon the previous example, let's create a dynamic table that includes a calculated column for calculating the profit margin for each product category:

1. Navigate to Data Modeling: In Power BI Desktop, navigate to the Modeling tab.

2. Create a New Table: Click on the New Table button.

3. Define Calculation: In the formula bar, define the calculation for the dynamic product table with the calculated profit margin column using the AVERAGEX and FILTER functions:

```DAX
DynamicProductTable =
ADDCOLUMNS(
    VALUES('Sales'[Product Category]),
    "Average Profit Margin",
    AVERAGEX(
        FILTER('Sales', 'Sales'[Product Category] = EARLIER('Sales'[Product Category])),
        'Sales'[Profit] / 'Sales'[Revenue]
    )
)
```

This DAX formula creates a dynamic table named 'DynamicProductTable' that lists all unique product categories and includes an "Average Profit Margin" calculated column.

4. Visualize Data: Drag and drop the 'Product Category' and 'Average Profit Margin' columns from the 'DynamicProductTable' onto a visualization, such as a table or chart. You can now visualize the average profit margin for each product category.

7.3.3 Leveraging User Interactions

Dynamic tables can be further enhanced by leveraging user interactions and selections.

Example: Dynamic Table with User-Selected Category

Let's modify the previous example to allow users to select a specific product category and display details about that category dynamically:

1. Navigate to Data Modeling: In Power BI Desktop, navigate to the Modeling tab.

2. Create a New Table: Click on the New Table button.

3. Define Calculation: In the formula bar, define the calculation for the dynamic table with user-selected product category using the SELECTEDVALUE and FILTER functions:

```DAX
DynamicProductDetails =
ADDCOLUMNS(
    FILTER('Sales', 'Sales'[Product Category] =
SELECTEDVALUE('DynamicProductTable'[Product Category])),
    "Product",
    'Sales'[Product],
```

```
    "Revenue",

    'Sales'[Revenue],

    "Profit",

    'Sales'[Profit]

)
```

This DAX formula creates a dynamic table named 'DynamicProductDetails' that displays details about the selected product category.

4. Visualize Data: Create a slicer visualization using the 'Product Category' column from the 'DynamicProductTable'. Then, create another visualization (e.g., table or card) using the columns from the 'DynamicProductDetails' table. As users select a product category from the slicer, the details will dynamically update based on the selection.

Dynamic tables provide a versatile way to perform calculations, generate customized views, and interact with data in Power BI. By mastering the creation of dynamic tables using DAX, you can create tailored analyses and visualizations that meet the unique needs of your business and empower more informed decision-making.

CHAPTER VIII
Combining DAX Functions

8.1 Nesting DAX Functions for Complex Calculations

In the world of Power BI and DAX, the ability to combine and nest functions is a fundamental skill that enables you to perform complex calculations and derive valuable insights from your data. Nesting involves using one DAX function within another, allowing you to create intricate formulas that cater to specific analytical requirements. This chapter will guide you through the art of nesting DAX functions, providing real-world examples and step-by-step instructions to master this essential technique.

Understanding Nesting and its Benefits

Nesting DAX functions involves using the output of one function as an input for another function. This approach is particularly valuable when dealing with complex calculations that require multiple steps. By breaking down the problem into smaller, manageable components and nesting functions, you can achieve sophisticated results without the need for overly convoluted formulas.

Example: Nested Calculations for Dynamic Discounts

Imagine you have a 'Sales' table with 'Product Price' and 'Discount Percentage' columns, and you want to calculate the discounted price for each product. Instead of creating a single formula, you can nest functions to achieve this:

```DAX
Discounted Price = 'Sales'[Product Price] * (1 - 'Sales'[Discount Percentage])
```

```
```

Here, the nested function involves multiplying the 'Product Price' by the result of the subtraction operation within the parentheses. This approach enhances readability and simplifies the formula.

Nesting Aggregation and Filter Functions

Nesting becomes particularly powerful when working with aggregation and filter functions, enabling you to perform calculations on a subset of data within a larger context.

Example: Calculating Weighted Average Revenue

Suppose you have a 'Customers' table with 'Revenue' and 'Segment' columns, and you want to calculate the weighted average revenue for each segment. Nesting the SUMX and FILTER functions achieves this:

```DAX
Weighted Avg Revenue =
SUMX(
   'Customers',
   'Customers'[Revenue] *
   CALCULATE(
      COUNTROWS('Customers'),
      FILTER('Customers', 'Customers'[Segment] = EARLIER('Customers'[Segment]))
   )
) / SUM('Customers'[Revenue])
```

In this nested calculation, the FILTER function restricts the rows to the current segment, and COUNTROWS returns the number of customers in that segment. The result is then used to weight the 'Revenue' in the SUMX function.

Combining Different Function Types

Nesting also enables the combination of different types of functions, such as logical and aggregation functions, to achieve intricate calculations.

Example: Calculating Churn Rate

Consider a 'Subscriptions' table with 'Start Date' and 'End Date' columns. To calculate the churn rate, you can nest the COUNTROWS and SUMX functions along with logical conditions:

```DAX
Churn Rate =
COUNTROWS(
  FILTER(
    'Subscriptions',
    'Subscriptions'[End Date] <= TODAY() &&
    'Subscriptions'[Start Date] <= EOMONTH(TODAY(), -1)
  )
) / SUMX('Subscriptions', IF('Subscriptions'[Start Date] <= EOMONTH(TODAY(), -1), 1, 0))
```

Here, the nested functions calculate the number of churned subscriptions and the total subscriptions, ultimately yielding the churn rate.

Step-by-Step Guide to Nesting DAX Functions

1. Identify the Calculation: Determine the complex calculation you need to perform, breaking it down into smaller logical steps.

2. Select Functions: Choose the appropriate DAX functions for each step of the calculation. Consider the inputs and outputs of each function.

3. Nest Functions: Insert one function inside another, using the appropriate syntax and considering the order of operations.

4. Test and Validate: Validate the nested formula by applying it to sample data and comparing results to expected outcomes.

5. Optimize: Refine and optimize the nested functions for performance and readability.

By mastering the art of nesting DAX functions, you unlock the potential to perform sophisticated calculations, analyze data from various angles, and gain deeper insights into your business metrics. The examples and techniques presented in this chapter provide a solid foundation for creating complex calculations that cater to your unique analytical needs.

8.2. Building Calculated Columns and Measures

Calculated columns and measures are essential tools in Power BI that allow you to create custom calculations based on your data. They enable you to extend your data model and perform complex calculations that go beyond what is possible with simple DAX functions alone. In this section, we will explore the concepts of calculated columns and measures, how they differ, and provide step-by-step guidance on how to create and use them effectively.

Understanding Calculated Columns and Measures

Calculated Columns: These are columns you add to a table in your data model. They use DAX formulas to calculate a value for each row in the table. Calculated columns are precomputed during data loading and become a permanent part of your data model. They are useful for calculations that involve row-level operations and provide context at the individual row level.

Measures: Measures, on the other hand, are calculations performed on the fly during query execution. They are typically used for aggregations, such as sums, averages, counts, etc. Measures are dynamic and provide results based on the current context of your report or visualization. They are stored as part of your data model's metadata and are not precomputed during data loading.

Creating Calculated Columns

To create a calculated column, follow these steps:

1. Open Power BI Desktop: Launch Power BI Desktop and load your data.

2. Navigate to Data View: Click on the "Data" view to see your data model.

3. Select the Table: In the "Fields" pane, select the table for which you want to create the calculated column.

4. Modeling Tab: Go to the "Modeling" tab in the ribbon.

5. New Column: Click on "New Column."

6. Enter Formula: In the formula bar, enter your DAX formula for the calculated column. For example, to create a calculated column for total revenue, you could use: `Total Revenue = Sales[Quantity] * Sales[Unit Price]`.

7. Press Enter: Press Enter to apply the formula.

8. Column Name: Rename the column to a meaningful name, like "Total Revenue."

9. Save: Save your changes.

Creating Measures

To create a measure, follow these steps:

1. Open Power BI Desktop: Launch Power BI Desktop and load your data.

2. Navigate to Data View: Click on the "Data" view to see your data model.

3. Modeling Tab: Go to the "Modeling" tab in the ribbon.

4. New Measure: Click on "New Measure."

5. Enter Formula: In the formula bar, enter your DAX formula for the measure. For instance, to calculate total sales, you could use: `Total Sales = SUM(Sales[Amount])`.

6. Press Enter: Press Enter to apply the formula.

7. Measure Name: Rename the measure to a descriptive name, such as "Total Sales."

8. Save: Save your changes.

Choosing Between Calculated Columns and Measures

The choice between calculated columns and measures depends on the nature of your calculation and your performance requirements. Consider the following guidelines:

- Use calculated columns when the calculation involves row-level operations and you need the result for each individual row.

- Use measures for aggregations, calculations that involve different levels of aggregation, or dynamic calculations based on user interactions.

Best Practices

- Optimize Performance: Avoid creating too many calculated columns, as they can increase memory consumption. Use measures for aggregations to enhance query performance.

- Documentation: Provide clear and meaningful names for your calculated columns and measures. Document their purpose and usage to ensure others can understand and use them effectively.

- Reuse: Whenever possible, reuse existing calculated columns and measures in your reports and visualizations to maintain consistency and save time.

By understanding the distinction between calculated columns and measures and following best practices for their creation and usage, you can harness the full power of DAX to perform advanced calculations and analysis within your Power BI projects.

8.3. Chaining Functions for Advanced Data Transformations

In the world of Power BI and DAX, the true power emerges when you start combining functions to create more intricate and sophisticated calculations. Chaining functions is a technique where the output of one function serves as the input for another, allowing you to perform multi-step calculations in a single DAX formula. This chapter explores the art of function chaining and provides practical examples to demonstrate how to achieve complex data transformations.

Understanding Function Chaining

Function chaining involves taking the output of one function and feeding it directly into another function. This is achieved by nesting functions within one another, with the inner function operating on the result produced by the outer function. This approach can significantly simplify your DAX code and make it more efficient.

Practical Examples of Function Chaining

Example 1: Calculating Weighted Average

Suppose you have a sales table with columns for sales amount and quantity sold. To calculate the weighted average sale price, you can use the AVERAGEX and SUMX functions:

```
Weighted Average = SUMX(Sales, Sales[Amount] * Sales[Quantity]) / SUMX(Sales, Sales[Quantity])
```

Here, the SUMX function calculates the sum of the product of sales amount and quantity for each row, and then divides it by the sum of the quantity column.

Example 2: Finding Percent of Total

To calculate the percentage of total sales for each category, you can chain the SUMX and DIVIDE functions:

```
Percent of Total = DIVIDE(SUMX(Sales, Sales[Amount]),
CALCULATE(SUM(Sales[Amount]), ALL(Sales)))
```

In this example, the SUMX function calculates the sum of sales amount for each category, and the CALCULATE function provides the total sales amount across all categories by using the ALL function.

Step-by-Step Guide to Chaining Functions

Let's walk through the process of chaining functions using the weighted average calculation as an example:

1. Open Power BI Desktop: Launch Power BI Desktop and load your data.

2. Navigate to Data View: Click on the "Data" view to see your data model.

3. Modeling Tab: Go to the "Modeling" tab in the ribbon.

4. New Measure: Click on "New Measure."

5. Enter Formula: In the formula bar, enter the chained DAX formula for the weighted average calculation:

```
Weighted Average = SUMX(Sales, Sales[Amount] * Sales[Quantity]) / SUMX(Sales, Sales[Quantity])
```

6. Press Enter: Press Enter to apply the formula.

7. Measure Name: Rename the measure to "Weighted Average."

8. Save: Save your changes.

Benefits of Function Chaining

Function chaining offers several advantages:

- Efficiency: Chaining functions can eliminate the need for intermediate calculated columns, making your calculations more efficient.

- Clarity: Chained functions can often lead to more concise and readable code, as you're performing multiple calculations in a single formula.

- Flexibility: Function chaining allows you to build complex calculations without cluttering your data model with additional columns.

Best Practices

- Test and Validate: Always test and validate your chained functions to ensure they produce the expected results.

- Use Comments: Include comments within your DAX formula to document the purpose and logic of each function.

- Start Simple: Begin with simple function chaining and gradually progress to more complex combinations as you become more comfortable with the technique.

Function chaining in DAX provides a powerful way to perform advanced data transformations and calculations in your Power BI projects. By mastering this technique, you can create sophisticated analyses that extract valuable insights from your data.

CHAPTER IX
Time Intelligence Functions in DAX

9.1 Introduction to Time Intelligence in Power BI

Time is a crucial dimension in data analysis, enabling us to uncover trends, patterns, and insights that might otherwise go unnoticed. Time intelligence functions in DAX provide a powerful toolkit for performing calculations and analyses related to time-based data. In this chapter, we'll delve into the world of time intelligence, exploring the concepts, functions, and techniques that will empower you to extract meaningful insights from your temporal data in Power BI.

Understanding Time Intelligence

Time intelligence refers to the ability to perform calculations and comparisons involving time-related data, such as dates, weeks, months, quarters, and years. It enables us to analyze data based on time periods, identify trends, and make informed decisions. Time intelligence functions are specifically designed to work with date and time values in DAX and provide a range of capabilities, from simple calculations like year-to-date sums to complex analyses involving moving averages, rolling totals, and more.

The Significance of Time Intelligence in Analysis

Time intelligence is essential for various scenarios, such as:

- **Comparative Analysis:** Compare data across different time periods to understand growth rates, trends, and changes.

- Period-over-Period Analysis: Analyze data for the same period in different years to identify seasonal patterns.

- Rolling Averages: Calculate moving averages to smooth out fluctuations and reveal long-term trends.

- Time-Shifted Comparisons: Analyze data with a time lag to understand how events in one period affect another.

Key Time Intelligence Functions

1. TOTALYTD

The TOTALYTD function calculates a measure's year-to-date total, considering the specified year-end date.

Example:
```
```
Total Sales YTD = TOTALYTD(SUM(Sales[Amount]), Dates[Date])
```
```

2. SAMEPERIODLASTYEAR

The SAMEPERIODLASTYEAR function returns a table that contains a parallel period in the previous year.

Example:

```

Sales LY = CALCULATE(SUM(Sales[Amount]), SAMEPERIODLASTYEAR(Dates[Date]))

```

3. DATESYTD

The DATESYTD function returns a table that represents the year-to-date period of a given date table.

Example:

```

Sales YTD = SUMX(DATESYTD(Dates[Date]), Sales[Amount])

```

Practical Example: Calculating Moving Averages

Suppose you have a dataset with daily sales data. To calculate a 7-day moving average for sales, follow these steps:

1. Create a New Measure: Go to the "Modeling" tab and create a new measure named "7-Day Moving Avg."

2. Enter DAX Formula: In the formula bar, enter the DAX formula using the AVERAGEX and DATESINPERIOD functions:

```
7-Day Moving Avg = AVERAGEX(DATESINPERIOD(Dates[Date],
LASTDATE(Dates[Date]), -7, DAY), Sales[Amount])
```

3. Press Enter: Press Enter to apply the formula.

4. Save Changes: Save your changes.

Benefits of Time Intelligence

Time intelligence functions empower you to perform dynamic and contextual analyses that adapt to user selections and changes in time frames. These functions enable you to derive valuable insights from your data, which are crucial for making informed business decisions.

Best Practices

- **Use a Dedicated Date Table:** Create a dedicated date table with relevant columns for efficient time-based calculations.

- **Understand Date Relationships:** Ensure proper relationships between your date table and other tables in the data model.

- **Consider Performance:** Some time intelligence functions can impact performance, so use them judiciously.

Time intelligence functions are a cornerstone of effective time-based analysis in Power BI. Mastering these functions will elevate your ability to uncover hidden trends and patterns in your data, leading to more accurate and insightful business decisions.

9.2. Working with TOTALYTD, TOTALQTD, and TOTALMTD Functions

In the world of data analysis, understanding and harnessing the power of time is crucial. Time intelligence functions enable you to perform complex calculations that involve time periods, allowing you to gain insights into year-to-date, quarter-to-date, and month-to-date data. In this section, we will explore the usage of three important time intelligence functions: TOTALYTD, TOTALQTD, and TOTALMTD. These functions are essential tools in your arsenal when it comes to understanding cumulative values over time periods.

Understanding Cumulative Totals

Cumulative totals are a fundamental aspect of time-based analysis. They help you track the accumulation of a measure over specific time intervals. The TOTALYTD (Total Year-to-Date), TOTALQTD (Total Quarter-to-Date), and TOTALMTD (Total Month-to-Date) functions provide a seamless way to calculate cumulative values while accounting for the context of time.

TOTALYTD: Total Year-to-Date

The TOTALYTD function calculates the total of a measure from the beginning of the year up to a specified date. This function is particularly useful for tracking year-to-date performance.

Syntax:

```
```

TOTALYTD(<expression>, <dates>, [<filter>])

```
```

- `<expression>`: The measure to be aggregated.

- `<dates>`: The date column to consider.

- `<filter>` (optional): An additional filter to apply.

Example:

Suppose you have a sales dataset with a "Sales" table and a "Date" table. To calculate the year-to-date total sales up to a selected date, use the TOTALYTD function:

```
```

Total Sales YTD = TOTALYTD(SUM('Sales'[Amount]), 'Date'[Date])

```
```

TOTALQTD: Total Quarter-to-Date

The TOTALQTD function calculates the total of a measure from the beginning of the quarter up to a specified date. This is useful for monitoring quarter-to-date progress.

Syntax:
```
```

TOTALQTD(<expression>, <dates>, [<filter>])

```
```

- `<expression>`: The measure to be aggregated.

- `<dates>`: The date column to consider.

- `<filter>` (optional): An additional filter to apply.

Example:

To calculate the quarter-to-date total sales up to a selected date, you can use the TOTALQTD function:

```
Total Sales QTD = TOTALQTD(SUM('Sales'[Amount]), 'Date'[Date])
```

TOTALMTD: Total Month-to-Date

The TOTALMTD function calculates the total of a measure from the beginning of the month up to a specified date. It is ideal for analyzing month-to-date performance.

Syntax:

```
TOTALMTD(<expression>, <dates>, [<filter>])
```

- `<expression>`: The measure to be aggregated.

- `<dates>`: The date column to consider.

- `<filter>` (optional): An additional filter to apply.

Example:

For calculating the month-to-date total sales up to a selected date, you can employ the TOTALMTD function:

```
```

Total Sales MTD = TOTALMTD(SUM('Sales'[Amount]), 'Date'[Date])

```
```

Practical Example: Tracking Quarter-to-Date Sales

Imagine you are analyzing quarterly sales performance using a sales dataset. To track quarter-to-date sales, follow these steps:

1. Create a New Measure: Navigate to the "Modeling" tab and create a new measure named "Total Sales QTD."

2. Enter DAX Formula: In the formula bar, enter the following DAX formula using the TOTALQTD function:

```
```

Total Sales QTD = TOTALQTD(SUM('Sales'[Amount]), 'Date'[Date])

```
```

3. Press Enter: Press Enter to apply the formula.

4. Save Changes: Save your changes.

Now, you have a measure that dynamically calculates the quarter-to-date total sales based on user selections.

Benefits of Using TOTALYTD, TOTALQTD, and TOTALMTD

These time intelligence functions offer several advantages:

- **Dynamic Analysis:** The functions adapt to user selections and provide context-aware calculations.

- **Consistency:** Regardless of filtering or data changes, these functions ensure accurate cumulative calculations.

- **Time-Saving:** The functions eliminate the need for complex manual calculations involving cumulative values.

Best Practices

- **Date Hierarchy:** Ensure your date table has a hierarchy (Year > Quarter > Month) for seamless time-based analysis.

- **Proper Filtering:** Use additional filters in the functions to narrow down calculations based on specific criteria.

- **Performance Consideration:** Like any DAX functions, be mindful of their impact on performance, especially with large datasets.

Mastering TOTALYTD, TOTALQTD, and TOTALMTD functions will empower you to explore time-based trends, analyze performance, and gain deeper insights into your data. By understanding how to effectively use these functions, you can confidently perform cumulative calculations and provide valuable insights to drive better business decisions.

9.3. Creating Custom Time Intelligence Functions

While DAX provides a rich set of built-in time intelligence functions, there might be instances where your analysis requires a custom approach. Creating custom time intelligence functions allows you to tailor your calculations to specific business needs, providing greater flexibility and precision. In this section, we will explore the process of designing and implementing your own custom time intelligence functions in DAX.

Identifying the Need for Custom Functions

Custom time intelligence functions come in handy when you encounter unique business scenarios that are not fully addressed by standard DAX functions. These scenarios might involve complex date calculations, non-standard fiscal calendars, or specific holiday adjustments. By creating custom functions, you can ensure that your analysis accurately reflects the intricacies of your business environment.

Steps to Create Custom Time Intelligence Functions

1. Define the Function's Purpose: Clearly outline the purpose of your custom time intelligence function. What specific calculation or adjustment is required that cannot be achieved with existing DAX functions?

2. Plan the Parameters: Determine the necessary parameters for your function. These could include input dates, reference periods, or any other values needed for your calculation.

3. Write the DAX Formula: In Power BI or any DAX-supported environment, open the formula bar and write your DAX formula. This formula will encapsulate the custom calculation you want to perform.

4. Test and Refine: Before deploying your custom function widely, test it thoroughly with different scenarios and datasets. Refine the formula as needed to ensure accuracy.

5. Create a Measure or Column: Depending on your use case, you can create a custom measure or calculated column that utilizes your custom function.

6. Documentation: Clearly document the purpose, parameters, and usage instructions for your custom function. This documentation is crucial for yourself and others who might work with your Power BI model.

Example: Calculating Custom Moving Averages

Let's say you need to calculate a custom moving average over a rolling six-month period, where each month's average includes data from the previous five months. This is not directly achievable with standard DAX functions. Here's how you could create a custom function for this scenario:

1. Define Purpose: Calculate a moving average over a custom rolling period.

2. Plan Parameters: Input date, column to average, and number of months in the rolling period.

3. Write DAX Formula: Use DAX functions like SUMX, FILTER, and EARLIER to create your custom moving average calculation.

4. Test and Refine: Test the function with different date ranges and validate results.

5. Create Measure: Create a new measure, e.g., "Custom Moving Average," and use your custom function in its formula.

6. Documentation: In your documentation, explain the formula, parameters, and provide examples of how to use the measure in different visuals.

Benefits of Custom Time Intelligence Functions

- Precision: Custom functions allow you to fine-tune calculations for your specific requirements.

- Flexibility: Address unique business scenarios that standard functions might not cover.

- Reusability: Once created, custom functions can be reused across multiple measures and visuals.

- Consistency: Ensure consistent and accurate calculations throughout your analysis.

Best Practices

- Simplicity: Keep your custom functions as simple as possible to avoid unnecessary complexity.

- Testing: Thoroughly test your custom functions with different scenarios to ensure accuracy.

- Documentation: Provide clear and comprehensive documentation for your custom functions.

Creating custom time intelligence functions empowers you to perform intricate analyses that cater to your organization's exact needs. By following the steps outlined here and leveraging your understanding of DAX, you can extend your analytical capabilities and provide more valuable insights to your stakeholders.

CHAPTER X
Advanced DAX Techniques

10.1 Understanding DAX Evaluation Context

In the realm of Data Analysis Expressions (DAX), grasping the concept of Evaluation Context is pivotal for mastering advanced techniques. Evaluation context defines how DAX calculations interact with data, filters, and relationships, influencing the results you obtain. In this section, we will delve deep into understanding the Evaluation Context in DAX and explore its significance through practical examples.

What is Evaluation Context?

Evaluation context refers to the set of filters, rows, and columns that are active at a particular point in a DAX formula's execution. It determines which data is included in the calculation and how relationships are applied. Mastering the concept of Evaluation Context allows you to craft intricate calculations that yield accurate and desired results.

Evaluation Context Components

1. Row Context: At the core of Evaluation Context is the row context. When a DAX formula is evaluated for each row in a table, the current row's data serves as the context for calculations.

2. Filter Context: Filters applied to a DAX formula restrict the data that is included in calculations. Filters can be explicit, such as user selections, or implicit, like relationships between tables.

3. Column Context: When calculations involve multiple columns, the column context influences how calculations propagate across the data model.

Impact on DAX Calculations

Understanding Evaluation Context is crucial because it affects the behavior of various DAX functions, especially those that iterate over tables or manipulate context. Functions like SUMX, AVERAGEX, and CALCULATE are particularly sensitive to Evaluation Context.

Practical Example: Total Sales for Each Product Category

Let's consider a scenario where you want to calculate the total sales for each product category. The formula would be:

```DAX
Total Sales by Category = SUMX(Products, Sales[Amount])
```

Here, the Evaluation Context involves iterating through each row in the Products table and calculating the total sales for the corresponding category in the Sales table.

Tips for Working with Evaluation Context

1. Use CALCULATE to Modify Context: The CALCULATE function allows you to change or override the current Evaluation Context. This is helpful when you want to apply filters temporarily.

2. Avoid Conflicting Contexts: Be cautious of conflicting Evaluation Contexts, which can lead to unexpected results. Understand how context transitions occur.

3. Utilize ROW and FILTER Functions: Functions like ROW and FILTER enable you to create custom Evaluation Contexts for specific calculations.

4. Practice and Experiment: Becoming proficient in managing Evaluation Context requires practice. Experiment with different scenarios to deepen your understanding.

Benefits of Mastering Evaluation Context

- **Precise Calculations:** Control over Evaluation Context ensures precise and targeted calculations.

- **Efficiency:** Properly managing context can lead to more efficient queries and faster performance.

- **Complex Analysis:** Advanced DAX calculations, such as time intelligence and advanced filters, rely heavily on accurate Evaluation Context management.

Conclusion

In the world of DAX, grasping Evaluation Context is akin to unlocking the full potential of your analytical toolkit. By mastering this fundamental concept, you gain the ability to craft intricate calculations and manipulate data contextually, ultimately leading to more accurate and insightful analyses in your Power BI reports and data models.

10.2. Context Transition in DAX: ROW, FILTER, and CALCULATETABLE

In the intricate world of Data Analysis Expressions (DAX), understanding context transition is akin to becoming a maestro in orchestrating data manipulations. Context transition involves the deliberate manipulation of Evaluation Context to achieve desired outcomes in calculations. In this section, we will explore three powerful DAX functions - ROW, FILTER, and CALCULATETABLE - that allow you to master context transition and wield advanced DAX techniques effectively.

Transitioning from Row Context to Filter Context

Before delving into the functions, it's crucial to grasp the concept of transitioning from row context to filter context. Row context pertains to calculations made at the granularity of individual rows, while filter context involves applying filters to shape the data set for calculations. Context transition shifts the focus from row-level calculations to a more holistic view of data.

10.2.1 Leveraging ROW for Context Transition

The ROW function enables you to create a virtual table with a single row and use it to manipulate context transitions. It's particularly useful for scenarios where you need to calculate measures at different levels of granularity. Let's consider an example:

Suppose you want to calculate the total sales for each product category and its subcategory. You can achieve this using the ROW function:

```DAX
Sales by Category and Subcategory =
```

```
SUMX(
    VALUES(Products[Category], Products[Subcategory]),
    [Total Sales]
)
```

Here, the VALUES function creates a virtual table with distinct values from both Category and Subcategory columns, effectively transitioning the context to the desired granularity.

10.2.2 Filtering with the FILTER Function

The FILTER function allows you to dynamically modify filter context within a DAX calculation. It's immensely powerful when you need to apply selective filtering based on specific conditions. Consider the following example:

Suppose you want to calculate the average sales amount for products that have sales exceeding $1,000. You can achieve this using the FILTER function:

```DAX
Average Sales for High-Value Products =
CALCULATE(
    AVERAGE(Sales[Amount]),
    FILTER(Sales, Sales[Amount] > 1000)
)
```

In this case, the FILTER function modifies the filter context by restricting the data to only include products with sales above $1,000.

10.2.3 Sculpting Context with CALCULATETABLE

The CALCULATETABLE function is a versatile tool for creating custom tables that define the context for calculations. It allows you to shape the filter context by specifying rows that should be included in the calculation. Let's illustrate this with an example:

Suppose you want to calculate the total sales for a specific date range. You can use the CALCULATETABLE function to create a custom date table and apply it to the Sales table:

```DAX
Total Sales in Q2 2023 =
CALCULATE(
    [Total Sales],
    CALCULATETABLE(
        Dates,
        Dates[Date] >= DATE(2023, 4, 1) && Dates[Date] <= DATE(2023, 6, 30)
    )
)
```

Here, the CALCULATETABLE function generates a custom table with dates in the specified range, effectively shaping the filter context for the calculation.

10.2.4 Best Practices for Context Transition

1. Understand the Context Transition: Ensure a solid understanding of how context transition works before applying advanced techniques.

2. Optimize Calculations: Context transition can impact performance. Use functions like ROW, FILTER, and CALCULATETABLE judiciously to strike a balance between accuracy and efficiency.

3. Test and Iterate: Experiment with different scenarios and iterate your calculations to fine-tune the results.

4. Documentation: Document the context transition logic for future reference and collaboration with your team.

Conclusion

Mastering context transition in DAX opens a new realm of possibilities for advanced calculations and analysis. The ROW, FILTER, and CALCULATETABLE functions empower you to manipulate Evaluation Context, transition between row and filter contexts, and sculpt custom contexts to achieve precise and dynamic results. Armed with these techniques, you'll be well-equipped to tackle complex scenarios and unlock deeper insights in your Power BI reports and data models.

10.3. DAX Optimization and Best Practices

In the intricate world of Data Analysis Expressions (DAX), mastering advanced techniques is only half the battle. To truly harness the power of DAX and create efficient, high-performing Power BI models and reports, it's essential to delve into optimization and adopt best practices. This section will guide you through the art of DAX optimization, offering practical tips, techniques, and best practices to ensure your DAX calculations run smoothly and deliver optimal performance.

10.3.1 Simplify Calculations with Measures

One of the fundamental principles of DAX optimization is to embrace the use of measures. Measures encapsulate complex calculations and prevent unnecessary recalculations. When designing your Power BI model, focus on creating measures for commonly used calculations, aggregations, and metrics. This not only enhances readability but also boosts performance by reducing redundant computations.

10.3.2 Minimize the Use of Calculated Columns

While calculated columns have their place in DAX, excessive use can impact model performance. Calculated columns are computed during data import and consume memory. Whenever possible, opt for measures instead of calculated columns, as measures are evaluated on the fly, utilizing memory more efficiently.

10.3.3 Avoid Expensive DAX Functions

Certain DAX functions are more resource-intensive than others. Functions like SUMX, AVERAGEX, and CALCULATE can introduce overhead, especially when applied to large datasets. Whenever feasible, explore alternative approaches or optimizations to achieve the same results. Consider using native aggregation functions like SUM and AVERAGE for better performance.

10.3.4 Optimize Filter Context

Context transition plays a pivotal role in DAX optimization. Efficiently managing filter context can significantly enhance performance. Utilize functions like FILTER and CALCULATETABLE strategically to shape and modify filter context only when necessary. Carefully evaluate whether context transition is required for specific calculations and avoid unnecessary modifications.

10.3.5 Manage Relationships Thoughtfully

Effective management of relationships within your data model is crucial for both accuracy and performance. Avoid creating redundant relationships, as they can introduce ambiguity and negatively impact calculations. Choose the appropriate relationship type (single or bi-directional) based on your data requirements. Regularly review and validate relationships to ensure they align with your analytical goals.

10.3.6 Leverage Query Folding

Query folding is a powerful technique that enables Power Query to push data transformations back to the data source. This minimizes data movement and processing, resulting in faster query performance. Whenever possible, design your Power Query transformations to allow query folding, optimizing data retrieval and transformation.

10.3.7 Monitor and Profile Performance

Regularly monitor and profile your DAX calculations and queries to identify performance bottlenecks. Utilize built-in tools like DAX Studio and Performance Analyzer in Power BI to pinpoint areas that require optimization. Addressing performance issues proactively ensures a smooth user experience and efficient report interaction.

10.3.8 Documentation and Collaboration

As you optimize your DAX calculations, document your decisions, optimizations, and best practices. This documentation not only serves as a reference for future development but also facilitates collaboration within your team. Share insights, techniques, and optimization strategies to collectively enhance the DAX expertise within your organization.

Conclusion

DAX optimization is both an art and a science, requiring a deep understanding of DAX functions, context transition, and data model architecture. By implementing the best practices outlined in this section, you can ensure that your Power BI models deliver exceptional performance while providing accurate and insightful analyses. Strive to strike a balance between functionality and efficiency, and continuously refine your DAX calculations to create a seamless and responsive end-user experience.

CHAPTER XI
DAX in Real-World Scenarios

11.1 Financial Analysis with DAX

In this chapter, we delve into the real-world application of Data Analysis Expressions (DAX) for financial analysis within Power BI. Financial analysis often involves complex calculations, aggregations, and comparisons, making it an ideal domain to harness the power of DAX. We will explore various DAX functions and techniques that enable you to perform a wide range of financial analyses, from basic metrics to advanced forecasting.

11.1.1 Calculating Key Financial Metrics

DAX provides an array of functions that are instrumental in calculating fundamental financial metrics. These metrics include:

Revenue and Profit Calculation

Use DAX functions like SUMX, FILTER, and CALCULATE to compute total revenue, net profit, and gross profit margins. For instance, to calculate net profit, apply the following formula:

```DAX
Net Profit = SUMX(Sales, Sales[Revenue]) - SUMX(Expenses, Expenses[Cost])
```

Return on Investment (ROI)

DAX can help you calculate ROI by considering initial investment and final value. Utilize DIVIDE and SUMX to calculate ROI percentage, as shown:

```DAX
ROI (%) = DIVIDE(SUMX(Investments, Investments[FinalValue] - Investments[InitialValue]), SUMX(Investments, Investments[InitialValue])) * 100
```

11.1.2 Time-Series Analysis and Forecasting

Time-series analysis is pivotal in financial forecasting. DAX empowers you to create dynamic time-based calculations for insights and predictions.

Moving Averages

Calculate moving averages for key financial metrics using DAX functions like AVERAGEX and FILTER. For instance, compute a 3-month moving average of monthly sales as follows:

```DAX
3-Month Moving Avg = AVERAGEX(
    FILTER(Sales, EARLIER(Sales[Date]) - 90 <= Sales[Date] && Sales[Date] <= EARLIER(Sales[Date])),
    Sales[Revenue]
)
```

Forecasting Future Values

Leverage DAX to forecast future financial values based on historical data. By combining functions like SUMX, FILTER, and ADDCOLUMNS, you can create custom forecasting models. Assume you want to predict next month's revenue using a simple linear regression:

```DAX
Forecasted Revenue = SUMX(
    Sales,
    [Slope] * MAX(Sales[MonthNumber]) + [Intercept]
)
```

11.1.3 Analyzing Financial Ratios

Financial ratios provide insights into a company's financial health. DAX facilitates the computation of various ratios, such as:

Current Ratio

Calculate the current ratio by dividing current assets by current liabilities:

```DAX
Current Ratio = SUMX(Assets, Assets[CurrentAssets]) / SUMX(Liabilities, Liabilities[CurrentLiabilities])
```

```
```

Debt-to-Equity Ratio

Use DAX functions to compute the debt-to-equity ratio, a measure of financial leverage:

```DAX
Debt-to-Equity Ratio = SUMX(Liabilities, Liabilities[TotalLiabilities]) / SUMX(Equity, Equity[TotalEquity])
```

11.1.4 Visualizing Financial Insights

Power BI's visualization capabilities complement DAX's analytical prowess. Create dynamic financial reports and dashboards by combining DAX measures with charts, tables, and slicers. Visualize financial trends, comparisons, and forecasts to provide actionable insights.

Line Charts for Revenue and Expenses

Construct line charts to showcase revenue and expense trends over time. Utilize DAX measures for accurate data representation and dynamic visualization.

KPI Cards for Key Metrics

Create Key Performance Indicator (KPI) cards to display essential financial metrics such as net profit, ROI, and current ratio. DAX measures enable real-time updates to KPIs as underlying data changes.

Conclusion

Financial analysis with DAX empowers finance professionals to transform raw financial data into actionable insights. By harnessing the capabilities of DAX functions and techniques, you can perform comprehensive financial analyses, create accurate forecasts, and visualize financial trends effectively. This chapter equips you with the knowledge and skills to leverage DAX in real-world financial scenarios, enhancing your ability to make informed decisions and drive financial success.

11.2. Sales and Revenue Insights with DAX

In this chapter, we explore the application of Data Analysis Expressions (DAX) in real-world scenarios, specifically focusing on analyzing sales and revenue data using Power BI. Sales and revenue analysis is a critical aspect of business decision-making, and DAX offers powerful tools to extract valuable insights from your data. We will walk through various DAX functions and techniques that enable you to perform comprehensive sales and revenue analysis, from basic calculations to advanced trend identification.

11.2.1 Calculating Sales Metrics

DAX provides an arsenal of functions that are invaluable in calculating essential sales metrics. These metrics include:

Total Sales Calculation

Use DAX's SUM function to calculate total sales for a given period. For instance, to calculate total sales for a specific year, use the following formula:

```DAX
Total Sales = SUM(Sales[Amount])
```

Average Sales per Customer

Leverage DAX's AVERAGE function to compute the average sales per customer. This can be particularly insightful for understanding customer spending patterns:

```DAX
Average Sales per Customer = AVERAGE(Sales[Amount])
```

11.2.2 Segmenting and Categorizing Sales Data

DAX enables you to segment and categorize sales data, allowing for deeper analysis and insights.

Sales by Product Category

Use DAX functions like SUMX and FILTER to calculate sales for each product category:

```DAX
Sales by Category = SUMX(FILTER(Sales, Sales[Category] = "Electronics"), Sales[Amount])
```

Sales by Region

DAX can help you analyze sales performance across different regions. Utilize CALCULATETABLE and VALUES to calculate sales by region:

```DAX
Sales by Region = SUMX(CALCULATETABLE(Sales, VALUES(Region)), Sales[Amount])
```

11.2.3 Identifying Sales Trends

DAX is instrumental in identifying sales trends and patterns over time.

Monthly Sales Growth

Calculate month-over-month sales growth using DAX functions like SUM and LAG:

```DAX
Monthly Sales Growth =
    (SUM(Sales[Amount]) - LAG(SUM(Sales[Amount]), 1)) / LAG(SUM(Sales[Amount]), 1)
```

Yearly Sales Comparison

Compare sales performance between different years using DAX's SAMEPERIODLASTYEAR function:

```DAX
Yearly Sales Comparison =
    SUM(Sales[Amount]) -
    CALCULATE(SUM(Sales[Amount]), SAMEPERIODLASTYEAR(Calendar[Date]))
```

11.2.4 Visualizing Sales and Revenue Data

Power BI's visualization capabilities complement DAX's analytical capabilities. Combine DAX measures with various charts and visualizations to create compelling sales and revenue dashboards.

Line Charts for Sales Trends

Create line charts to visualize sales trends over time. Use DAX measures to ensure accurate representation of sales data.

Stacked Bar Charts for Category Analysis

Generate stacked bar charts to analyze sales distribution across different product categories. DAX measures enhance the accuracy of category-wise sales visualization.

Conclusion

Sales and revenue insights derived from DAX-driven analysis empower businesses to make informed decisions, optimize strategies, and drive growth. By harnessing the capabilities of DAX functions and techniques, you can uncover valuable sales trends, segment data effectively, and create compelling visualizations. This chapter equips you with the skills to leverage DAX in real-world scenarios, enabling you to extract meaningful insights from sales and revenue data and contribute to the success of your organization.

11.3. Customer Behavior Analysis using DAX

Understanding customer behavior is paramount for businesses aiming to enhance customer experiences, tailor marketing strategies, and optimize sales processes. In this section, we delve into the application of Data Analysis Expressions (DAX) for customer behavior analysis using Power BI. We'll explore various DAX functions and techniques that allow you to gain valuable insights into customer interactions, preferences, and purchasing patterns.

11.3.1 Customer Segmentation

DAX provides powerful tools for segmenting customers based on their behaviors and characteristics.

High-Value Customers

Identify high-value customers by calculating their total purchases. Use DAX to filter and aggregate data:

```DAX
High-Value Customers =
  FILTER(
```

```
    SUMMARIZE(

        Customer,

        Customer[Name],

        "Total Purchases", SUM(Sales[Amount])

    ),

    [Total Purchases] > 10000

)
```

New vs. Returning Customers

Use DAX to determine the ratio of new to returning customers:

```DAX
New vs. Returning Customers =
    DIVIDE(
        COUNTROWS(
            FILTER(
                Customer,
                [First Purchase Date] = [Current Date]
            )
        ),
        COUNTROWS(Customer)
    )
```

```
```

11.3.2 Purchase Patterns Analysis

DAX facilitates the analysis of customer purchase patterns, aiding in product recommendations and inventory management.

Average Days Between Purchases

Calculate the average number of days between a customer's purchases:

```DAX
Average Days Between Purchases =
  AVERAGEX(
    SUMMARIZE(
      Customer,
      Customer[Name],
      "Days Between Purchases", [Min Days Between Purchases]
    ),
    [Days Between Purchases]
  )
```

Frequently Bought Together

Leverage DAX to identify products frequently bought together by customers:

```DAX
Frequently Bought Together =
  TOPN(
    5,
    SUMMARIZE(
      Sales,
      Sales[Product A],
      Sales[Product B],
      "Total Sales", SUM(Sales[Amount])
    ),
    [Total Sales],
    DESC
  )
```

11.3.3 Churn Prediction

Predicting customer churn is vital for retention efforts. DAX can aid in churn prediction models.

Churn Rate Calculation

Calculate the churn rate using DAX functions like COUNTROWS and FILTER:

```DAX
Churn Rate =
  DIVIDE(
    COUNTROWS(
      FILTER(
        Customer,
        [Last Purchase Date] < [Churn Date]
      )
    ),
    COUNTROWS(Customer)
  )
```

11.3.4 Visualizing Customer Behavior

Combine DAX measures with Power BI visualizations to create insightful dashboards.

Customer Segmentation Pie Chart

Visualize customer segments using a pie chart. Utilize DAX measures to classify customers into segments.

Purchase Patterns Heatmap

Create a heatmap to display purchase patterns. DAX measures help in aggregating and categorizing data for accurate visualization.

Conclusion

Customer behavior analysis powered by DAX empowers businesses to tailor their strategies, enhance customer experiences, and make informed decisions. By utilizing DAX functions and techniques, you can gain valuable insights into customer segmentation, purchase patterns, churn prediction, and more. This chapter equips you with the skills to leverage DAX in real-world scenarios, enabling you to decipher customer behavior patterns and drive positive business outcomes.

CHAPTER XII
Future Trends in DAX and Power BI

12.1 Evolving Landscape of DAX and Analytics

In the fast-paced world of data analytics, staying attuned to emerging trends and technologies is crucial. As we explore the future landscape of Data Analysis Expressions (DAX) and its integration with Power BI, it becomes apparent that exciting developments are shaping the field. This chapter delves into the evolving trends and strategies that are likely to impact DAX and analytics in the coming years.

12.1.1 Rise of AI and Machine Learning

Artificial Intelligence (AI) and Machine Learning (ML) are on an upward trajectory, and their convergence with DAX is poised to revolutionize data analysis. Power BI's integration with AI capabilities empowers users to employ predictive analytics, anomaly detection, and natural language processing in their datasets. For instance, the use of AI-driven algorithms can enhance customer behavior predictions, optimize inventory management, and facilitate dynamic forecasting.

Implementation Example: Predictive Sales Forecasting

Imagine a retail company using historical sales data. By combining DAX functions with AI algorithms, Power BI can predict future sales figures, enabling the company to make informed decisions about inventory, staffing, and marketing efforts.

12.1.2 Data Governance and Compliance

With increasing data privacy concerns and regulations like GDPR and CCPA, data governance and compliance are gaining prominence. DAX and Power BI are evolving to provide enhanced data protection features, ensuring that sensitive information is handled securely.

Implementation Example: Masking Personal Identifiable Information (PII)

Consider a scenario where a financial institution analyzes customer spending patterns. DAX can be utilized to mask PII like names and contact details, preserving privacy while performing valuable analysis.

12.1.3 Enhanced Natural Language Processing (NLP)

The ability to interact with data using natural language is transforming how users engage with analytics platforms. Power BI's integration of advanced NLP capabilities offers a more intuitive way to query and understand data.

Implementation Example: Conversational Analytics

An organization could use Power BI to build a chatbot interface that allows users to ask questions and receive insights using natural language. DAX functions can process these queries and return relevant visualizations.

12.1.4 Cloud-Centric Analytics

Cloud computing is reshaping the analytics landscape, providing scalability, accessibility, and real-time collaboration. Power BI's integration with cloud services allows seamless data sharing and collaborative analysis.

Implementation Example: Real-Time Collaboration

Multiple users can simultaneously work on a Power BI dashboard hosted in the cloud. DAX calculations can be performed in real-time, enabling dynamic discussions and joint decision-making.

12.1.5 Advanced Data Modeling

Future trends suggest a focus on advanced data modeling techniques that harness the full potential of DAX. Enhanced data relationships, multi-dimensional modeling, and semantic layer development are expected to become more prevalent.

Implementation Example: Multidimensional Sales Analysis

A retail company might create a multidimensional data model in Power BI, incorporating DAX functions to analyze sales across various dimensions like time, region, and product categories, providing deeper insights.

Conclusion

The future of DAX and Power BI holds exciting possibilities as these technologies continue to evolve. The integration of AI, improved data governance, enhanced NLP, cloud-centric analytics, and advanced data modeling will shape the way organizations approach data analysis and decision-making. By staying informed about these trends and actively incorporating them into your DAX and Power BI practices, you can unlock new levels of insights and drive your analytics initiatives to greater heights.

12.2. AI and Machine Learning Integration in DAX

Artificial Intelligence (AI) and Machine Learning (ML) are revolutionizing the field of data analysis, and their integration with Data Analysis Expressions (DAX) holds immense potential for driving deeper insights and predictive capabilities in Power BI. This section explores how AI and ML are being seamlessly integrated into DAX to enhance data analysis and decision-making.

12.2.1 The Synergy of DAX and AI/ML

The marriage of DAX with AI and ML brings a new dimension to data analysis. DAX, with its rich set of functions for calculations and transformations, can now leverage the predictive and pattern recognition capabilities of AI/ML algorithms. This synergy enables analysts and data professionals to uncover hidden insights and forecast trends with unprecedented accuracy.

12.2.2 AI-Driven Forecasting with DAX

One of the most compelling applications of AI integration in DAX is forecasting. Traditional forecasting methods often rely on historical trends, but AI-driven forecasting can adapt to complex and dynamic data patterns. By combining DAX's time intelligence functions with AI algorithms, Power BI users can create models that automatically adjust predictions based on changing variables.

Implementation Example: Sales Forecasting

Suppose a retail company wants to forecast future sales based on historical data. By integrating AI algorithms into DAX calculations, Power BI can generate forecasts that account for factors like seasonality, economic trends, and even external events such as holidays or promotions.

12.2.3 Sentiment Analysis and Natural Language Processing (NLP)

AI-powered sentiment analysis and NLP can be seamlessly integrated into DAX to analyze text data and gauge public sentiment. DAX functions can preprocess and prepare the text data for analysis, while AI models interpret the sentiment behind customer reviews, social media mentions, and other unstructured data.

Implementation Example: Social Media Sentiment Analysis

An organization can utilize DAX to prepare social media text data for analysis. AI models can then be employed to determine the sentiment behind each post or comment, helping businesses gauge public perception and tailor their strategies accordingly.

12.2.4 Anomaly Detection and Outlier Analysis

AI-powered anomaly detection can be combined with DAX to identify unusual patterns or outliers in data. This integration enhances the ability to detect anomalies in time series data and trigger alerts or actions based on predefined thresholds.

Implementation Example: Fraud Detection

For a financial institution, DAX can preprocess transaction data while AI algorithms detect unusual spending patterns indicative of fraud. The combination of DAX's data manipulation capabilities and AI's pattern recognition enhances fraud detection accuracy.

12.2.5 Personalized Recommendations

Integrating AI and ML into DAX enables the creation of personalized recommendation systems. By analyzing user behavior and preferences, DAX functions can collaborate with AI algorithms to suggest products, content, or actions tailored to individual users.

Implementation Example: E-Commerce Recommendations

DAX can gather customer interaction data on an e-commerce platform. By integrating AI and ML, the system can then generate personalized product recommendations, improving user engagement and potentially driving sales.

12.2.6 Implementation Steps

1. Identify AI/ML Use Cases: Determine which AI/ML applications can enhance your data analysis tasks. This could include forecasting, sentiment analysis, anomaly detection, or personalized recommendations.

2. Data Preparation with DAX: Use DAX functions to clean, transform, and preprocess your data. Ensure that the data is in a suitable format for AI/ML algorithms.

3. Integrate AI/ML Libraries: Utilize AI/ML libraries or services (such as TensorFlow, scikit-learn, or Azure ML) to develop the necessary models for your use case.

4. Combine DAX and AI/ML: Integrate the AI/ML predictions or classifications into your DAX calculations. This may involve creating new measures, columns, or tables that incorporate the AI/ML outputs.

5. Testing and Validation: Thoroughly test and validate the integrated solution to ensure accuracy and reliability.

Conclusion

The integration of AI and Machine Learning into DAX opens up a world of possibilities for data analysts and professionals. By combining the analytical power of DAX with the predictive capabilities of AI/ML, organizations can extract deeper insights, make more accurate forecasts, and deliver personalized experiences to users. As this integration continues to evolve, the boundary between traditional data analysis and advanced AI-driven insights will blur, leading to more informed decision-making and a competitive edge in the data-driven landscape.

12.3. Predictive Analytics with DAX

Predictive analytics is a powerful approach that utilizes historical data, statistical algorithms, and machine learning techniques to identify the likelihood of future outcomes. Integrating predictive analytics with DAX opens up a world of possibilities for businesses to make data-driven decisions, anticipate trends, and gain a competitive edge. In this chapter, we'll explore how to harness the predictive capabilities of DAX within Power BI for various real-world scenarios.

12.3.1 Understanding Predictive Analytics

Predictive analytics involves creating models that can forecast future events based on historical data. These models use advanced algorithms to identify patterns, relationships, and anomalies in the data, enabling organizations to anticipate changes and make proactive decisions. By integrating predictive analytics with DAX, Power BI users can leverage their existing data and calculations to develop accurate predictive models.

12.3.2 Implementing Predictive Analytics with DAX

To demonstrate the implementation of predictive analytics using DAX in Power BI, let's consider a scenario where we want to predict customer churn based on historical customer data.

Step 1: Data Preparation

1. **Data Collection**: Gather historical customer data, including attributes such as customer demographics, purchase history, and interactions.

2. **Data Cleaning and Transformation:** Use Power Query to clean and transform the data, ensuring it's suitable for analysis.

Step 2: Feature Engineering

1. **Identify Relevant Features:** Determine which features are likely to influence customer churn, such as customer age, purchase frequency, and customer support interactions.

2. **Create DAX Measures:** Use DAX to create new calculated columns or measures that aggregate or transform the data. For example, calculate the average purchase frequency for each customer.

Step 3: Model Building

1. **Choose Predictive Model:** Select a suitable predictive model for customer churn prediction, such as logistic regression, decision trees, or random forests.

2. **Train the Model:** Split the data into training and testing sets. Use the training set to train the predictive model on historical data.

Step 4: Integrating Predictive Model with DAX

1. **Prediction Using DAX:** Create a DAX formula that utilizes the trained predictive model to calculate the probability of customer churn for each customer based on their attributes and historical behavior.

2. Incorporate Predictions: Integrate the predictions into your Power BI reports by creating visuals that display the likelihood of customer churn for different customer segments.

12.3.3 Benefits of Predictive Analytics with DAX

Integrating predictive analytics with DAX offers several advantages:

1. Data Utilization: Leverage existing data and calculations in Power BI for predictive modeling, eliminating the need to switch between different tools.

2. Accuracy: Incorporate domain-specific knowledge into predictive models by combining DAX calculations with machine learning algorithms.

3. Real-time Insights: Continuously update predictions in real-time as new data becomes available, enabling timely decision-making.

4. Holistic Analysis: Combine historical analysis with future predictions to gain a comprehensive understanding of trends and potential outcomes.

12.3.4 Future Directions

The integration of predictive analytics with DAX is a stepping stone to more sophisticated AI-driven forecasting and modeling within Power BI. As advancements in AI and machine learning continue, we can expect even more seamless integration, automated model selection, and enhanced predictive capabilities.

Conclusion

Predictive analytics has the potential to revolutionize the way businesses operate by enabling proactive decision-making. The integration of predictive analytics with DAX empowers Power BI users to unlock valuable insights from their data and make accurate predictions. By following the outlined steps and examples, users can harness the combined power of DAX and predictive analytics to address complex business challenges, anticipate trends, and drive success in the data-driven era. As this integration evolves, organizations will be better equipped to navigate uncertainties, optimize processes, and create a future of informed possibilities.

Appendix
DAX Function Reference

A.1 Common DAX Functions and Syntax

In this appendix, we provide a comprehensive reference guide to common DAX functions along with their syntax, descriptions, and practical examples. These functions serve as the building blocks for creating powerful calculations and analyses within Power BI. By understanding how to use these functions effectively, you'll be equipped to handle a wide range of data transformations and calculations.

NOTE: This reference is not exhaustive, but it covers a selection of fundamental DAX functions to get you started.

1. SUM Function

Syntax: SUM(column)

Description: Calculates the sum of a numeric column.

Example: Calculate the total sales amount for a given period.

```DAX
Total Sales = SUM(Sales[Amount])
```

2. AVERAGE Function

Syntax: AVERAGE(column)

Description: Calculates the average of a numeric column.

Example: Calculate the average revenue per customer.

```DAX
Average Revenue = AVERAGE(Customer[Revenue])
```

3. COUNT Function

Syntax: COUNT(column)

Description: Counts the number of rows in a column.

Example: Count the number of orders placed.

```DAX
Total Orders = COUNT(Orders[OrderID])
```

4. MIN Function

Syntax: MIN(column)

Description: Returns the smallest value in a column.

Example: Find the minimum temperature recorded.

```DAX
Min Temperature = MIN(Weather[Temperature])
```

5. MAX Function

Syntax: MAX(column)

Description: Returns the largest value in a column.

Example: Find the maximum revenue generated.

```DAX
Max Revenue = MAX(Sales[Revenue])
```

6. CALCULATE Function

Syntax: CALCULATE(expression, filter1, filter2, ...)

Description: Modifies the filter context of a calculation by applying additional filters.

Example: Calculate the total sales for a specific region.

```DAX
Total Sales North = CALCULATE(SUM(Sales[Amount]), Sales[Region] = "North")
```

7. FILTER Function

Syntax: FILTER(table, condition)

Description: Creates a table that includes only the rows that meet the specified condition.

Example: Filter products with sales above a certain threshold.

```DAX
High Sales Products = FILTER(Products, Products[Sales] > 1000)
```

8. RELATED Function

Syntax: RELATED(table[column])

Description: Returns a related column value from another table.

Example: Retrieve the customer name for a given order.

```DAX
Customer Name = RELATED(Customer[Name])
```

9. IF Function

Syntax: IF(condition, value_if_true, value_if_false)

Description: Returns one value if a condition is true and another value if it's false.

Example: Classify sales as "High" or "Low" based on a threshold.

```DAX
Sales Classification = IF(Sales[Amount] > 1000, "High", "Low")
```

10. YEAR Function

Syntax: YEAR(date)

Description: Returns the year part of a date.

Example: Extract the year from an order date.

```DAX
Order Year = YEAR(Orders[OrderDate])
```

11. MONTH Function

Syntax: MONTH(date)

Description: Returns the month part of a date.

Example: Extract the month from a transaction date.

```DAX
Transaction Month = MONTH(Transactions[Date])
```

12. CONCATENATE Function

Syntax: CONCATENATE(text1, text2, ...)

Description: Combines multiple text strings into one.

Example: Create a full name by concatenating first and last names.

```DAX
Full Name = CONCATENATE(Customer[First Name], " ", Customer[Last Name])
```

13. LEFT Function

Syntax: LEFT(text, num_chars)

Description: Returns a specified number of characters from the beginning of a text string.

Example: Get the first three characters of a product code.

```DAX
Product Code Prefix = LEFT(Products[Product Code], 3)
```

14. RIGHT Function

Syntax: RIGHT(text, num_chars)

Description: Returns a specified number of characters from the end of a text string.

Example: Get the last four digits of a phone number.

```DAX
Phone Number Suffix = RIGHT(Customer[Phone], 4)
```

15. LEN Function

Syntax: LEN(text)

Description: Returns the number of characters in a text string.

Example: Count the number of characters in a product description.

```DAX
Description Length = LEN(Products[Description])
```

This DAX Function Reference provides you with the foundational knowledge needed to start working with DAX in Power BI. By mastering these functions and understanding their syntax, you can perform various calculations, create measures, and transform your data to gain valuable insights and make informed decisions. As you become more comfortable with these basic functions, you'll be well-equipped to explore more advanced DAX techniques and unleash the full analytical potential of Power BI.

A.2 Advanced DAX Functions and Combinations

In this appendix, we delve into more advanced DAX functions and explore how they can be combined to solve complex data analysis challenges. These functions enable you to perform intricate calculations, create dynamic measures, and enhance your insights within Power BI. By mastering these advanced techniques, you'll gain a deeper understanding of DAX's capabilities and be better equipped to handle sophisticated analytical tasks.

1. SUMX Function

Syntax: SUMX(table, expression)

Description: Calculates the sum of an expression for each row in a table.

Example: Calculate the total revenue by summing up the product of sales quantity and unit price.

```DAX
Total Revenue = SUMX(Sales, Sales[Quantity] * Sales[Unit Price])
```

2. RANKX Function

Syntax: RANKX(table, expression, [value], [order], [ties])

Description: Assigns a rank to each row based on the specified expression.

Example: Rank products based on their total sales.

```DAX
Product Rank = RANKX(Products, [Total Sales])
```

3. EARLIER Function

Syntax: EARLIER(expression, [column])

Description: Refers to a column value in an outer evaluation context when used in an iterator function.

Example: Calculate the difference between the current sales and sales from the previous year.

```DAX
Sales Growth = [Total Sales] - EARLIER([Total Sales], Date[Year])
```

4. ALL Function

Syntax: ALL(table, [column1], [column2], ...)

Description: Removes filters from a table or specified columns.

Example: Calculate the total sales regardless of any applied filters.

```DAX
Total Sales (No Filters) = CALCULATE([Total Sales], ALL(Sales))
```

5. DIVIDE Function

Syntax: DIVIDE(numerator, denominator, [alternate_result])

Description: Divides two numbers and handles division by zero gracefully.

Example: Calculate the profit margin using the divide function.

```DAX
Profit Margin = DIVIDE([Total Profit], [Total Revenue], 0)
```

6. SWITCH Function

Syntax: SWITCH(expression, value1, result1, [value2, result2], ... [default_result])

Description: Evaluates an expression against multiple values and returns the corresponding result.

Example: Categorize products based on their sales ranges using the switch function.

```DAX
Sales Category =
SWITCH([Total Sales],
    [Total Sales] < 1000, "Low",
    [Total Sales] < 5000, "Medium",
    [Total Sales] >= 5000, "High",
    "Unknown"
)
```

7. TOPN Function

Syntax: TOPN(count, table, expression, [order], [ties])

Description: Returns the top N rows based on a specified expression.

Example: Retrieve the top 10 customers based on their total purchases.

```DAX

Top Customers = TOPN(10, Customers, [Total Purchases], DESC)

```

8. SUMMARIZE Function

Syntax: SUMMARIZE(table, [groupby_column1], [groupby_column2], ..., [expression1], [expression2], ...)

Description: Creates a summary table with specified grouping columns and expressions.

Example: Create a summary table with total sales and average revenue per product category.

```DAX
Category Summary = SUMMARIZE(Products, Products[Category],

    "Total Sales", [Total Sales],

    "Avg Revenue", [Average Revenue]

)
```

9. CONCATENATEX Function

Syntax: CONCATENATEX(table, delimiter, expression)

Description: Concatenates text values in a column, separated by a delimiter.

Example: Create a comma-separated list of products within a category.

```DAX
Products List = CONCATENATEX(Products, ", ", Products[Product Name])
```

10. DATESBETWEEN Function

Syntax: DATESBETWEEN(date_table, start_date, end_date)

Description: Returns a table of dates between the specified start and end dates.

Example: Calculate sales for a specific date range.

```DAX
SalesInRange = SUMX(DATESBETWEEN(Date, [Start Date], [End Date]), [Total Sales])
```

By exploring these advanced DAX functions and learning how to combine them effectively, you'll be well-prepared to tackle complex analytical scenarios and unlock deeper insights from your data. These techniques empower you to create custom calculations, dynamic measures, and intricate data transformations, enhancing the value and depth of your Power BI reports and analyses. As you continue to experiment with these functions and incorporate them into your projects, you'll gain the expertise needed to drive more informed and impactful decision-making processes.

CONCLUSION

In this comprehensive journey through the world of DAX and Power BI, we've embarked on an exploration of data analysis expressions, their functions, and their integration within the powerful Power BI platform. We've covered the fundamental building blocks, from basic functions to advanced techniques, to help you master the art of transforming raw data into meaningful insights.

Throughout this book, we've dived deep into the intricacies of DAX functions, logical expressions, time intelligence, aggregation, and more. We've equipped you with the tools to handle real-world scenarios, enabling you to perform financial analysis, uncover sales patterns, analyze customer behavior, and even predict future trends. You've gained the expertise to combine functions, create calculated columns and measures, and navigate the evaluation context to achieve precise results.

As you've progressed through each chapter, you've not only acquired a solid understanding of DAX and Power BI, but you've also honed your analytical skills and problem-solving abilities. You're now equipped to leverage the full potential of DAX and Power BI to unearth hidden insights and guide data-driven decisions.

We extend our sincere gratitude to you, our valued reader, for embarking on this learning journey with us. Your dedication and commitment to mastering these essential skills are truly commendable. Remember that the world of data analysis is ever-evolving, and the knowledge you've gained from this book will serve as a strong foundation for your continued growth and success.

As you move forward, we encourage you to apply the concepts and techniques learned here to real-world projects, further refining your abilities and contributing to the world of data-driven insights. We look forward to witnessing the impact you'll make in your field using the knowledge you've gained from "DAX Essentials: Mastering Data Analysis Expressions in Power BI."

Thank you for choosing this book, and we wish you the very best on your journey to becoming a proficient DAX and Power BI practitioner. May your analytical endeavors lead to a future enriched with meaningful discoveries and informed decisions.

Happy analyzing!

www.ingramcontent.com/pod-product-compliance
Lightning Source LLC
Chambersburg PA
CBHW080555060326
40689CB00021B/4860